ANOINTED
TO WIN

ANOINTED TO WIN

LIBERTY TURNIPSEED

While the author has made every effort to provide accurate internet addresses at the time of publication, neither the publisher nor the author assumes any responsibility for errors or for changes that occur after publication. Further, the publisher does not have any control over and does not assume any responsibility for author or third-party websites or their content.

Visit the author's website at spiritmoveministry.co.

Cataloging-in-Publication Data is on file with the Library of Congress.

International Standard Book Number: 978-1-63641-237-5
E-book ISBN: 978-1-63641-238-2

23 24 25 26 27 — 987654321
Printed in the United States of America

Most Charisma Media products are available at special quantity discounts for bulk purchase for sales promotions, premiums, fund-raising, and educational needs. For details, call us at (407) 333-0600 or visit our website at www.charismamedia.com.

CONTENTS

FOREWORD

I HAVE BEEN IN the ministry since the early seventies and had never heard of the spirit of failurism. So when I received a copy of this book, my first question was, What is the spirit of failurism? Liberty does a great job explaining what the spirit of failurism is and how it affects us and those around us. But the most powerful thing about this book is that it doesn't just expose the problem but walks us through the solution.

Throughout the book, Liberty gives us opportunities to pray for our own deliverance from failurism. As I read her explanations, revelations, scriptures, and examples of the spirit of failurism at work, I realized that I had seeds of that spirit trying to take hold of me personally. So I prayed the prayers she has included in the book. Now I'm alert to the functions and strategies of the evil spirit trying to derail me from my purpose and cause me grief in my day-to-day life.

The second half of the book teaches us the importance of realizing Jesus alone is our righteousness. As a pastor and a prophet, Liberty is a good teacher of the Word. Her teaching on the righteousness of Christ and how to apply it to our lives in such a practical manner is outstanding. She even shares how she handles her own devotional time and encourages each of us to "do something" or "do something more" with regard to our own personal time with God. Simply refreshing!

This book will lead you through the understanding of what the spirit of failurism is, how you can deal with it in your personal life, and what practical steps you can take to protect yourself from it. It also explains the importance of knowing that Jesus alone is our righteousness! Enjoy! Then share with a friend!

—APOSTLE STEPHEN STRADER
IGNITED CHURCH, LAKELAND, FL
IGNITEDCHURCH.COM

INTRODUCTION

*F*AILURISM! WOW, THAT'S a loaded word. My hope in writing this book is based on my own experiences and personal revelations given to me through the Holy Spirit's guidance. It is to see people set free from the stronghold of failurism through my ministry. I have taken many through the deliverance process of breaking the stronghold of failurism in their lives. I was also delivered from this stronghold. The Lord gave me knowledge and revelation about this stronghold, and I could write a book with all the testimonies of those set free, with their lives forever changed. Failurism is a real spirit and a stronghold. You won't find this book full of fancy terminology or personal guidance I give through a one-on-one Christian counseling session.

My heart is to present you with this knowledge and revelation. Imagine I'm sitting at your table, enjoying a cup of coffee with you while I share my testimony of this stronghold and how it can be defeated in your life. My heart and passion for writing this book are to take you on a journey to show the thought process created and how it becomes our way of living as we allow ourselves to be bound by the spirit of failurism; show how to be delivered and set free from this demonic stronghold; and bring awareness to the reality that failurism is a spirit and that there's a war happening in the spiritual realm. But we cannot win the battle and be set free and defeat failurism without understanding the thought process that causes us to be bound in this stronghold. I will also explain how we can open the door wide for other smaller demons to attach themselves. They work within this major stronghold, and it's the actual process the devil attempts to take you through with lies and deception so that failurism becomes a way of life for you.

I will break it down into the manifestations that the Lord has revealed to me. I don't want to go too much into my testimony because I will be sharing it later in the book. I will say that when the Lord revealed the revelation to me that failurism was a spirit, I instantly sought the Lord's guidance and asked Him, "How it is a spirit, how does it work, and what are its manifestations?" That spirit immediately began to attack me, and I had to walk myself through self-deliverance. Had I not walked myself through that, I would have nothing to share with you in this book. Not only did I walk through it, but I also taught my entire church about the stronghold and walked them through it. This stronghold has now been added to our Deliverance Handbook and protocol for Restoration Ministries, a ministry that I founded. I can now walk you through it from my personal experience of feeling, knowing, seeing, and learning to understand just how strong this stronghold is in our lives and how easy it is to be deceived by it. My prayer is that when you finish this book, you will no longer walk in failurism. You will have the tools and the understanding to break free from this demonic stronghold. Will you still fail? Of course. You're human. But you don't have to live in it as a way of life.

CHAPTER 1

WHAT IS FAILURISM?

WE'VE ALL FAILED sometime in our lives; that's a given. We've all battled with making mistakes, maybe huge mistakes or poor choices. Failing is a normal part of life. No one can do everything perfectly, and we all learn as we go. The problem is when we choose to live in that place of failing. At different times in our lives, we all have figured out some things we're just not good at and some things we do very well. The reality is it's disappointing and discouraging when we fail—although we can't grow unless we've experienced failure. The problem is if we stay in disappointment and discouragement over failure, the spirit of failurism can come. The Lord gave me a series of messages about failurism, and I taught the congregation where I am the lead pastor. God was very clear that although there are no technical or proper definitions for the word *failurism*, it is a real issue. God has His own meaning and explains how failurism is real and exists.

So here's my story. Let me share with you how the Lord revealed all this to me.

I was sitting on my front porch in my regular favorite

1

spot where I do devotion early every morning. In my usual morning routine, I do my regular devotion and ask the Lord throughout the week, "What would You like me to speak about this week? What is on Your heart?" I always ask Him to share with me when He's ready, as I never want my devotion time to be all about preparing my next message to release. I want to focus on my daily growth, so I usually present this question to the Lord, and He faithfully answers me when He is ready. It commonly happens on Tuesday morning. On this particular Tuesday morning, I spent a lot of time with Him, and I said, "Lord, what message do You have for me to release this week? What do our people need to hear from You?"

He said to teach them about failurism, and I said, "Failurism?"

He said, "Yes, failurism, the spirit of failurism."

"Lord, is failurism a spirit?"

He said, "Yes, it is a stronghold with many manifestations. My people need to be made aware of this, and it must be broken off their lives."

Before we get technical and dive into the supernatural, let's talk about the word *failure*. What does *failure* mean? *Merriam-Webster* defines *failing* as "a usually slight or insignificant defect in character, conduct, or ability."[1] It defines *failure* as "a state of inability to perform a normal function…a fracturing or giving way under stress…a falling short…one that has failed."[2] *Vine's Expository Dictionary* defines *fail* as to "fall short."[3]

As I stated above, we have all failed and fallen short. That is why we need our Savior, Jesus Christ. He provides salvation so we don't have to live in failure, shame, guilt, and the condemnation that comes with them. I don't want to get ahead of myself because we will be talking about the symptoms and manifestations later. The reality is if you have read your Bible and are familiar with it, there are many stories of people, men and women of God, who failed big time.

Throughout this book, we will talk about some of those stories; those in the Bible failed in ways we can't even fathom. My goal is to help you understand that we have all failed. If you have failed in any form, you are in good company. Adam and Eve, Moses, King David, Solomon, Samson, Abraham and Sarah, and Saul of Tarsus, whom we know as Paul in the New Testament, are just a few that failed several times, made huge mistakes, and did evil in the sight of God.

Now, let's look at *failurism* as a complete word, although *failurism* doesn't have a proper official definition. Let's look at the word *ism*. I love the *Merriam-Webster* dictionary's definition of *ism*: "an oppressive and especially discriminatory attitude or belief."[4]

Wow, that blows my mind, and it should blow yours too. So let's look at the connection with *-ism* being added to the word *failure*. It provides more clarity and a more accurate description than the typical definition of the word *failure*.

Let's continue looking at a different dictionary version of *-ism*. Here's the Urban Dictionary's definition:

"Someone who does a distinctive specified thing so much, that they are now notorious for it. They are generally referred [to] as a 'their name'-ism."[5]

We've all been there. Everyone has failed in some way in their lifetime and will continue to fail. If you're reading this book, your goal is to break free from failurism in your life, the spirit, and the symptoms attached to it. It's crucial that we not be in denial of the fact that we have failed and we will continue to fail. *Fail* seems like such a strong word and can sound harsh, but the reality is we have all failed many, many times! We have all said and done things we should not have. We all have had to walk in a place of repentance and humility throughout our lives. It is common for us to have grief or a form of suffering or guilt, or to beat ourselves up for a short period when failing. The problem is we can't live in that failure. What happens if we continue walking in a state of failing, failurism, or believing the lie that the enemy has told us about ourselves because we have failed? We open the door for the demonic realm to wreak havoc in our lives.

When you think about the word *failurism*, you're probably thinking, "OK, you've told me the definition of *failure*, and you've told me the meaning of the word *ism*, but what does this word even mean when we put it together? What is failurism?"

When I was preparing to teach our church members and Connect Groups about failurism and its strongholds, this is the definition the Lord gave me: "Failurism is the state of continually walking in past sins, mistakes, and the rejection that came from those areas where you previously failed. You live as though you will always fail and be rejected, and it becomes your way of life." Those caught in the deceptive stronghold of failurism don't even realize they are caught in it. When we stay in a state of failurism, we open the door to the demonic realm and allow oppressive spirits to come in and attach to us. Then we become best friends with the spirit of failurism. Once we've allowed this spirit to attach to us, it begins to manifest in different ways in our lives. We create habits and patterns in our lives that control how we think, what we do, and what we don't do. We build lives around lies and deception from this attached spirit.

In turn, this opens the door for other oppressive demonic spirits and strongholds to deceive you and play on those new patterns created. The failurism spirit will use the already-made demonic weaknesses in your personality and characteristics learned throughout your life. Those demonic weaknesses become a vehicle for the lesser demons brought in by the spirit of failurism, and then those things become a way of life for you. Your reality and thought processes are not given to you by God. They build up in your mind; they are learned behaviors and reactions you have created for your life through the influence of the spirit of failurism, including all the manifestations of this major stronghold.

I've explained failurism, but you're probably asking, "What is the spirit of failurism?" The spirit of failurism is a demon sent by Satan to taunt you and remind you of your past, annoy you in your present, and ruin and halt your future. It will continue to tell you that you have made no progress, and are never going to be able to change and be different. It plants in your mind the idea that even if you repent, you are not forgiven, and you will always fail, no matter how much you try. This demon believes that if it highlights that as humans we fail and that we will fail again in some form, it can influence you to continue to live under the weight of failurism. This demon will continue to taunt you relentlessly by reminding you of your past. You become so frustrated in your present that you can't find the strength to move forward in any direction. This is what I mean by reminding you of your past, annoying you in your present, and ruining and halting your future.

All this demonic activity originates from Satan; however, this is a particular demon the Lord revealed to me with a specific assignment attached to it. Its particular job is to keep you from ever having a future in Christ, following the call, or finding out what your giftings are. It's not worrying whether you're saved and trying to steal your salvation. It's more concerned with keeping you so weighed down and frustrated with constantly battling this unseen enemy that you can't find even a glimmer of hope for your future. Therefore, your salvation in Christ and the new life you have in Him can never play out in your life and can never be seen or lived out because the power has been stripped away. The power of the cross can change your life, but the demon's end result is to keep you complacent and frustrated so you can never move forward to accomplish all that Christ has called you to perform while on this earth. We were all given a purpose from the time we were created in our mother's womb. And this demon helps the enemy, Satan, keep us from ever finding or walking in that purpose—because if we do, we could change the world for Christ and His kingdom on the earth.

Another main tactic of the spirit of failurism is to make us focus on our ability and power or strength. Jesus alone is our righteousness, and the power of the cross and the Holy Spirit is sufficient.

Let me share a story of a gentleman bound up by this demon. We will call him John. I walked John through deliverance and the removal of this demonic stronghold from his life. John was a middle-aged man around fifty-five years old who had been through a very rough divorce thirteen years before his deliverance. John was raised in the church, walked away from God as a teen, and fell into drugs, alcohol, and abuse. At a church event at around twenty years old, he was radically saved and delivered from drugs and alcohol. He joined the army and began his Christian walk; he then met his wife, was married, and felt God was calling him into ministry. Shortly after, John started seminary and graduated with his BA in theology. Things were going great. He and his wife had several children, and he began to serve in ministry in the army and help plant churches in various locations.

Another pastor serving in the army became his mentor and took John under his wing to train him in ministry. He continued for years being a father to him in the Lord. Years later, John was pastoring as a lead pastor and planting churches with continued spiritual support from his mentor. But after twenty-five years of marriage, John's wife came to him with a devastating blow. She was leaving him and wanted a divorce because she was in love with and in a relationship with his mentor.

The news crushed John and sent him straight into the arms of failurism. He could no longer serve in ministry and walked away from the call. As you can imagine, he went through many different feelings and emotions, but failurism was the biggest one he faced. He had failed his wife and his family. He tried everything to restore and reconcile, but John could not repair his marriage. His wife chose to marry his mentor, who was also married and left his wife for this new relationship. John eventually remarried a few years later, but he had a tremendous amount of baggage. He was full-on manifesting all the symptoms of the stronghold of failurism. He was angry, controlling, and a perfectionist. There was no room for failing at all. He was deflecting his insecurities onto his new family.

About five years ago, John and his new family ended up at our church and ministry. I founded Restoration Ministry, where we walk people through deliverance and inner healing. Before John was taken through his personal deliverance session, he learned about the stronghold of failurism through my teaching at the church. It was a fierce battle, and he was making some headway with the awareness of the stronghold by what he had learned, although the attachment did not want to go. Restoration Ministry has a team of prayer leaders I have personally trained to walk people through deliverance. During our sessions, we usually have a group of intercessors walk around the room or building to pray in the spirit and intercede for the prayer leader and the person being taken through deliverance. On John's day of deliverance I chose to walk John through his deliverance session as I knew we were facing a giant.

During John's session, I began to take him through the removal of a few lesser demons that needed to go first in preparation for the removal of the stronghold, failurism. As we prayed, those interceding walked around the room and were about ten to twenty feet away. Several rooms around us opened to the room where we were doing his session. I began to walk him through the removal of the spirit of failurism, and it came time for me to break the yoke; it was a powerful moment! John said he could feel a weight lift off him and leave at once. John described it like a heavy wet blanket on him. At the time I broke the yoke, one of our intercessors, who was about twenty feet away in another room but could hear what was happening, said she felt a thick wave of the glory of the Lord come from where we were sitting. She said it hit her in the face and almost knocked her to the floor, and she could barely stand under the weight of the glory. This story shows the reality of the spirit of failurism and that it is a real stronghold.

Let's read:

> And I, when I came to you, brothers, did not come proclaiming to you the testimony of God with lofty speech or wisdom. For I decided to know nothing among you except Jesus Christ and him crucified. And I was with you in weakness and in fear and much trembling, and my speech and my message were not in plausible words of wisdom, but in demonstration of the Spirit and of power, so that your faith might not rest in the wisdom of men but in the power of God.
>
> —1 CORINTHIANS 2:1–5

Paul explained to the Corinthians that power is found in Christ and His crucifixion. The devil is so sly and deceptive that he wants us to be self-righteous and focus on our own ability to be or do right. We must understand our faith rests in Christ's power, not our own. It will never come from our own sources of power or strength.

For fun, I like to look at different Bible versions for effect. Let us look at the same passage but in *The Message*:

> You'll remember, friends, that when I first came to you to let you in on God's sheer genius, I didn't try to impress you with polished speeches and the latest philosophy. I deliberately kept it

plain and simple: first Jesus and who he is; then Jesus and what he did—Jesus crucified. I was unsure of how to go about this, and felt totally inadequate—I was scared to death, if you want the truth of it—and so nothing I said could have impressed you or anyone else. But the Message came through anyway. God's Spirit and God's power did it, which made it clear that your life of faith is a response to God's power, not to some fancy mental or emotional footwork by me or anyone else.

—1 CORINTHIANS 2:1–5, MSG

I love how *The Message* put it. In the end, everything will be God's Spirit and God's power; no fancy footwork on our part will be necessary or could genuinely be effective in our lives for real growth and freedom. Once you truly know the manifestations, signs, and symptoms of the spirit of failurism and understand this one key point that Jesus alone is your righteousness, you can break the spirit of failurism entirely in your life. I will explain this in more detail in a later chapter that will be dedicated to what it means to walk in Jesus' righteousness. For now, I want this opening chapter to focus on your understanding of what failurism is. The spirit of failurism is real, exists, and is a stronghold and a demon sent out by the enemy to destroy your future and calling. As we delve in, I will outline the manifestations of the spirit of failurism and how the symptoms and signs begin in your life. It will be in the order the manifestations begin to show themselves that the Holy Spirit gave me as I was in preparation and prayer to teach on this subject. Let's dig in!

PART I

THE MANIFESTATIONS OF THE SPIRIT OF FAILURISM

CHAPTER 2

THE FUNNY THING ABOUT DECEPTION—IT'S DECEIVING

As we begin to walk ourselves through the manifestations of the spirit of failurism, deception is first and foremost the primary influence. Deception is what it is deceiving. Deception plays a lead role in the other manifestations that we will talk about throughout this book. A person cannot fall into the trap of failurism or the manifestations that come with the spirit of failurism without first being deceived.

What exactly is deception? According to the *Merriam-Webster*, *deception* means "the act of causing someone to accept as true or valid what is false or invalid; the act of deceiving...the fact or condition of being deceived... something that deceives; trick."[1]

International Standard Bible Encyclopedia says that *deceive* "denote[s] some deliberate misleading in the moral or spiritual realm."[2] Some examples of those who deceive are false teachers, false prophets, and Satan. Deception plays a key role in being led astray. We are led to believe what's being told to us by the enemy. We are being deceived, leading to our living our lives in deception.

The spirit of failurism works through deception. It attempts to trick you into continuing to believe the lies that the stronghold is trying to build up in your mind. Once the spirit of deception has attached itself to your mind and begins to make you believe that you are a failure and have failed, you stop trying and stop believing what is true about you and the life God has for you. Let's look at Revelation and see what it says about the enemy and how he works on this earth:

> And the great dragon was thrown down, the age-old serpent who is called the devil and Satan, he who continually deceives and seduces the entire inhabited world; he was thrown down to the earth and his angels were thrown down with him.
> — REVELATION 12:9, AMP

Satan's goal is to deceive you completely. If he can get you to believe that you're a failure and focus on your past sins and mistakes, then you very easily become open to the spirit of failurism becoming a stronghold in your life. The problem with deception is it's deceiving, as I stated earlier. Due to that, most people do not know that they are deceived—period. There are many false religions and false beliefs globally, and many people follow those false religions and false beliefs. Most people who follow those beliefs have no idea that they've been deceived. The Holy Spirit is the only One to help you recognize when you are walking in deception. People caught in false religions and belief systems that are not based on the Holy Spirit's guidance will have difficulty being set free or recognizing whether what they believe is true or false.

Here is a less severe and very lighthearted example of how easy deception can be, even in a nonspiritual sense. I have three sons, and when they were young, anytime I was not well and too sick to cook dinner, I usually asked my husband to cook for the family. My three sons were under the assumption (deceived) that because Mama was the one who always cooked, when Daddy cooked, it would not taste good, no matter how well my husband could cook. My boys believed that because I was the one who usually did the cooking, I was the only one who knew how to do it and make it taste good. We all know that is not true, but my boys were deceived into believing that's how it was. No matter how much I told them the food was fine, it was edible, and Daddy knows how to cook, they didn't believe and were afraid to eat it. Even if my husband cooked it precisely the same as I would have and followed the recipe to a T, our boys still believed it would not taste good. This is a funny example of how easy it is to be deceived and live in that deception.

Breaking the spirit of failurism, defeating it in our lives, and recognizing how deception plays a role is very serious. It is no laughing matter, but this example shows just how easy it is to be deceived and possibly spend years in deception. That was a physical example and not necessarily spiritual, but it paints a picture of literally how deception can play out.

First, you base your decisions and thought processes on what you've seen with your eyes, just like my boys had only seen Mama cooking most of the time, so they were already being deceived by what they saw with their eyes. It turned into a belief system that Mama was the only one who could make food taste good, and—now we're getting into the spiritual side—they did not trust their Daddy to present them with what he said he would give them.

Hopefully, you see where I'm going with this. When you fail, you are deceived into believing what you see in the physical realm. We will fail because our feelings and thoughts are based on what we see—just like my boys assumed my husband couldn't cook because they rarely saw him do it. We are deceived into thinking that's how it is; all life has to offer is failure and a second-rate meal, and we believe the lie. The enemy tells us about ourselves while God has and is trying to present us with salvation through His shed blood on the cross. No matter how much my husband would try to tell our boys that what he offered them was edible, they could not trust, believe, or accept it.

That is what happens when you fail and believe the lie. You become deceived, walk in deception, and can never accept what God has been trying to tell you and has offered you, period. You stop trusting the Bible's word that He has provided as a light to show us how to have salvation, receive it, and walk in it, or let it play out in our lives. Father God has already made it clear in His Word that we are in Him. Deception will keep you from realizing who you are in Him and allow the spirit of failurism to continue to manifest in your life.

How do you know if you are deceived or walking in deception? Here's the test. Are you lining up everything you think about yourself with the Word of God? Are you lining it up with what the Word says about you and what Christ has done for you? The Word of God is the final authority. Second Timothy 3:16–17 says, "All scripture is breathed out by God and profitable for teaching, for reproof, for correction, and for training in righteousness that the man of God may be complete, equipped for every good work."

Before we move on from this chapter, it's crucial that you recognize whether you are walking in deception. You must be willing and open to accept that it's possible you were and are deceived. Otherwise, as we go through these manifestations, you might not be able to recognize them in your life. You must identify deception in your life and the thought processes that come with it.

DELIVERANCE FROM THE SPIRIT OF DECEPTION

Say this prayer out loud with your hands held high.

Dear heavenly Father, I pray that deception will be removed from my mind, heart, and thoughts as I continue reading this book. I will see clearly what You are trying to say to me and what You are trying to show me in my life. I rebuke and bind the spirit of deception and command it to take its hands off me in the name of Jesus Christ of Nazareth, and I released truth to be activated in my mind, heart, and thoughts, in the name of Jesus Christ. Amen.

CHAPTER 3

WHAT, GOD?

HAVE YOU EVER thought, "What, God?" After deception, one of failurism's first manifestations or symptoms is to stop trusting God. It's very subtle, and we don't even realize we're doing it. We don't even know we have lost all trust in God and what He has previously said about us and our lives. Most people don't even realize that they're not believing and trusting in God the way they once did. They're led around by the spirit of failurism, and every decision is based on a life of failure. After this spirit has deceived you, you don't believe anything God said to you previously. Although you would not say this out loud or choose to believe that you've lost all trust and faith in the Lord, you have; it's very subtle.

> Trust in the LORD with all your heart, and do not lean on your own understanding. In all your ways acknowledge him, and he will make straight your paths.
>
> —PROVERBS 3:5–6

Once the spirit of failurism has got you going in other directions, working to fill a void or feed the feelings within you that you have been deceived into believing, you think you now have to work to earn God's love or work to continue to be loved by God. We continue to fill that void with work to create a comfort zone to feed the spirit of failurism.

We tell ourselves that if we do these specific things, it will keep us from failure. We stop trusting who God is in our lives, resulting in our working and moving. Then, all our decisions are based on a lack of trust in God, and we are no longer allowing the Holy Spirit to lead us. We are led by our fears of measuring up and begin to feel as if we have something to prove.

> May the God of hope fill you with all joy and peace in believing, so that by the power of the Holy Spirit you may abound in hope.
> —ROMANS 15:13

In this verse, Paul is encouraging us to stay filled with the hope that is in Christ Jesus and Him alone so that we abound in hope by the power of the Holy Spirit and the help of the Holy Spirit. What happens when we lose trust in God and do everything by our works? We no longer walk in the power of the Holy Spirit or allow God's presence to fill us with hope so that we can walk in joy and keep believing and trusting in what He has said and what

He has for us. We are now doing everything in our own strength, and living like that will not last long. We are not called to do anything in our own power, but if we continue to allow failurism to lead us and continue to feed the lie, we wear ourselves out, which will lead to the next manifestation of the spirit of failurism.

CHAPTER 4

I JUST CAN'T DO THIS ANYMORE

WHAT HAPPENS WHEN a car runs out of gas or a watch battery dies? The vehicle stops running or breaks down on the side of the road, and the watch stops working. This is the same thing that happens to us when we continue to try to walk in our own strength and not by the power of the Holy Spirit, as we talked about in the previous chapter. This is what leads to the next manifestation, which is you stop trying, you don't see a point in trying anymore, and you give up. You want to quit, but the reality is you have brought yourself to this place because of the lack of trust in the Lord, so now you are tired, burned out, worn out, sick, ill, stressed out, and possibly having other side effects such as infirmity, sickness, or you name it. The list grows and grows and grows.

When we get to a place where we completely give up because we've worn ourselves out, it is a severe spiritual condition to be in. When we are tired from going and going and going in our own strength because we've stopped trusting God, we open the door for the devil to come in other forms and attack us, and we welcome other oppressive spirits to attach to us. We leave ourselves vulnerable to going deeper into failurism.

> For it is [not your strength, but it is] God who is effectively at work in you, both to will and to work [that is, strengthening, energizing, and creating in you the longing and the ability to fulfill your purpose] for His good pleasure.
> —Philippians 2:13, amp

Paul is telling the Philippians that Christ is their strength. He will keep them going and give them what they need so they will never give up or quit or stop trying. The Holy Spirit is the One who energizes and strengthens us. Failurism wants us to keep going in our own strength until we wear ourselves sick. Once we get this far into the oppression of the spirit of failurism, a downward spiral continues because we have come to a place of being so tired and complacent, and we have opened the door to many things that we welcome rather than trying to stop them. We're giving demons free rein to come in and take us deeper into bondage.

> John answered them all by saying, "As for me, I baptize you [only] with water; but One who is mightier [more powerful, more noble] than I is coming, and I am not fit to untie the strap of His sandals [even as His slave]. He will baptize you

[who truly repent] with the Holy Spirit and [you
who remain unrepentant] with fire."
— LUKE 3:16, AMP

John is speaking of the true baptism, fire baptism, and
of course, water baptism, which is a significant step in
the salvation walk. Christ brought a baptism of fire. This
fire is made available to all who have received Christ in
their hearts, and this is the power we have to continue
our walks or calls without giving up. However, when we
don't use the power available to us, the strength that Paul
talks about in Philippians can never truly work in our
lives. The Holy Spirit and fire are the power behind that
strength that Paul talks about, and burnout comes very
quickly when we are working in our own strength.

God told me to write this book two years ago, but I
kept putting it off—but not because I didn't think it was
important to obey God or get this message out so people
could be set free. I'm a lead pastor and a church planter,
and I created Restoration Ministry, a deliverance and
inner healing ministry that God called me to start, along
with having a prophetic ministry that God called me to
come out of hiding and go public with. The battle was
on and challenging, which slowed down the start of this
book. I kept having a bursting forth in my spirit, and I
kept asking God, "What are You doing NOW?" That's
when I had several dreams that I was pregnant again.

The first prophetic dream I had in which I was pregnant

was in 2013, ten months after having a full radical hysterectomy (removal of both uterus and ovaries) at age thirty-five. Of course, I knew this was prophetic because I physically could not bear any more children. God was obviously telling me I was pregnant with a spiritual gift, calling, or ministry. Later, I was called to plant a Spirit-filled church in the community where God had recently moved us. Fast forward, and the pregnancy dreams were about my prophetic and deliverance ministries being birthed.

Then I had another pregnancy dream. It had been rough a couple of years before this. Satan fought hard to stop everything by using sickness, two severe car accidents with significant injuries to recover from, my father's death, and other things. It had been about seven or eight months since my last pregnancy dream, and I had a dream around 3:00 a.m. of sitting down and holding my pregnant belly. Suddenly, my water broke, and I looked down and said the baby was coming. I woke up and journaled it in my notepad. (I encourage you to journal your dreams, as God speaks through our dreams. They are not all from the pizza!)

I went back to sleep and got up at my usual time. During my prayer time, I asked God, "What could I possibly be pregnant with now? What's happening?" As I said earlier, I could feel I needed to release something. I felt as if I would burst at the seams, and I asked God, "Is this the book?" I had previously thought I needed to prepare and did an online writing class with Apostle Ryan LeStrange in preparation. In my spirit, I felt it was this book, but I needed another confirmation because I was already inundated and didn't want to be distracted if it wasn't God's timing.

The following morning, God woke me around 4:00 a.m. with a simple vision: "Scribe Arise." I knew then that the book was the baby I was getting ready to deliver. As many of you know, having a baby is painful. As soon as I decided to start this book, the war was on with the devil! This time it wasn't just attacks of sickness, etc. The devil went big. A Jezebel arose in our church to destroy it using someone we would have never believed. It came from nowhere, and the Jezebel attack blindsided us. Even with all that pain and betrayal, the devil wasn't done.

Our lead intercessor—who headed our pre-service prayer ministry, was our secretary/bookkeeper, and ran the prayer chain ministry, and whom I trained and raised in ministry—turned on our church. She decided she didn't believe in anything we were teaching and did not support the vision of the church as a whole. We were heartbroken and horrified! All of our leaders were crushed with betrayal and rejection.

I tell you all this because the devil fought hard to make me give up, quit, and believe the lies. I could have said I couldn't handle the heat and not written this book. But I did write, and it was only because of the Holy Spirit and fire.

There's one thing I didn't mention above about the woman who was my protégé. She joined forces with Jezebel to destroy all of God's work and our ministry, and it was evil at work. You need to be aware that she had been deceived. All her actions came from deception once she stopped trusting God, gave up, quit, and joined the demonic side. Isn't that scary? The Holy Spirit and sitting in His presence are what kept me going. I had every reason to quit and surrender so the attacks would stop. Instead, I went to people I looked up to and trusted for prayer. They blessed and helped strengthen me so that I would not give up. The power of the Holy Spirit is key, and you hold the key, but when you quit or give up, failurism increases its hold.

I've never been tested more by the spirit of failurism until I agreed with God to write this book. When the attack got so heavy and complex, it became stupid, just stupid, but the Holy Spirit gave me the strength to laugh at the devil and kick failurism in the face and continue writing.

CHAPTER 5

I DON'T WANT TO LOOK

WHEN YOU HAVE given up and quit trying, you move right into self-hate and begin to hate yourself. Why? Because deep inside, you feel like a loser, even though you chose to stop trying or fighting, and you hate yourself for doing it. Self-hate is a big issue because it leads to many other wrong thought processes about yourself, making it harder to be set free or break failurism off of your life. Failurism has deceived you into living as a failure, you've stopped trusting God and have given up, and now you hate yourself. The devil loves this and wants you to see no value in who you are and who God created you to be; this can literally destroy the call of God on your life. You begin to judge yourself according to your failure instead of who God has said you are.

Let's look at Psalm 139:13–18 (AMP):

> For You formed my innermost parts; You knit me [together] in my mother's womb. I will give thanks and praise to You, for I am fearfully and wonderfully made; wonderful are Your works,

and my soul knows it very well. My frame was
not hidden from You, when I was being formed
in secret, and intricately and skillfully formed [as
if embroidered with many colors] in the depths
of the earth. Your eyes have seen my unformed
substance; and in Your book were all written the
days that were appointed for me, when as yet
there was not one of them [even taking shape].
How precious also are Your thoughts to me, O
God! How vast is the sum of them! If I could
count them, they would outnumber the sand.
When I awake, I am still with You.

God knew who we were before we were even formed in
the womb. A very deadly manifestation of failurism can
lead to attempted suicide or suicide. It's imperative to recognize that the spirit of failurism is attacking us. Jesus died
before He knew us, and He died while we were sinners.

But God clearly shows and proves His own love
for us, by the fact that while we were still sinners,
Christ died for us.

—ROMANS 5:8, AMP

Jesus can redeem us from anything we have done. He
died for us even in the midst of our sinful lifestyles, so to
believe that God judges us the same way we judge ourselves is total deception! We are fearfully and wonderfully
made, which means all can be redeemed through Jesus

Christ. We mustn't allow ourselves to sink low, especially low enough to bring harm to ourselves. God loves us and has a beautiful plan. He doesn't promise the plan will be easy, but He never hates us or wishes He did not create us. There's always room for redemption. Jesus can redeem any mistakes we've made or areas in our lives where we have failed. He can turn everything for our good. It's important to know how significant a role the stronghold of failurism holds in self-hate. Being set free from the spirit of failurism can eradicate self-hate.

PRAYER FOR
DELIVERANCE FROM THE SPIRIT OF SELF-HATE

Say this prayer out loud with your eyes open:

> *Lord, I repent for partnering with the spirit of self-hate; please forgive me in the name of Jesus Christ. Amen. I renounce the spirit of self-hatred. I break all contracts previously made with this spirit in the name of Jesus Christ of Nazareth.*

Lay hands on yourself and repeat this prayer:

> *I break the yoke of self-hatred off of my life, and I command you to leave in the name of Jesus Christ. Amen. I release the truth of who I am in Christ to take the place where self-hatred resided!*

CHAPTER 6

I CAN'T DO ANYTHING

THIS MANIFESTATION IS simple. We blame ourselves if something isn't perfect. We literally make anything—and everything—about us, which is selfish and creates a host of other problems we won't go into here. We continue to spiral down once we've gotten to where we see everything from the vantage point of ourselves being the center and everything being about us. We're always blaming ourselves if something doesn't go right, and the entire time it never had anything to do with us. Still, the reality is that once you've gotten this deep, there's just no going back until you're delivered and set free from the spirit of failurism and you learn how to break it off of your life. Once again, you will stop trying and not see a point in making an effort because you have now taught yourself to become self-reliant rather than relying on the Holy Spirit. You will see life through the lens of who's to blame. In some circumstances, there is no one to blame. It's just life or the attacks of the enemy.

It's so important to be set free from constantly blaming ourselves or others because that is a very self-absorbed way of thinking. Several things will happen when you live attempting to place blame. As I said, deception is deceiving, and if the devil can make you so focused on yourself, you make no effort to go forward. You will exalt yourself or blame others to avoid feeling like a failure. The spirit of failurism makes you think that if you blame others, you will feel better. I call that false relief, and it is another lie of the enemy.

We must recognize the selfishness involved in blaming ourselves. It can seem very self-sacrificing, but really it's a pity party, and the devil just laughs because he's hoping that you will genuinely go deeper into failurism and just give up altogether. The devil is hoping that you will see absolutely no value in the part of you that has *not* failed. Usually, failure in the physical sense brings a tremendous growth period. We can't grow unless we fail sometimes. But the devil wants us to focus on the failing, for then we expect ourselves to be perfect, we don't try, or we give up. We have decided that our value is found in doing everything perfectly and not in our relationship with Christ and who He has created us to be. Trying to do everything perfectly feeds the spirit of failurism; attempting to do everything perfectly feeds the belief that things will never be accepted by God or anyone else unless they are done perfectly. It's a lie that feeds into the next manifestation of the spirit of failurism.

CHAPTER 7

WET BLANKET

W**HAT DOES IT** mean to be depressed? It means that the spirit of failurism has brought you to a place where you now open the door to the spirit of heaviness, and the spirit of heaviness lays on you like a wet blanket and weighs you down. Usually depression will cause you to feel as if you can't do anything. It literally steals your strength. You have gotten to the point where you're deceived. You see no point in trying now, and you hate yourself. You feel as if you can't accomplish anything, especially if it doesn't turn out perfectly.

If something does turn out perfectly, it will prove to you that you're not a failure, but the reality is you don't need to do something perfectly for you to have value or find value in yourself—value is found through Jesus Christ alone. It's crucial that you know, realize, and acknowledge that depression is a spirit of heaviness. I'm not going to preach to you about not taking medication, nor will I tell you to stop taking your medication. I will tell you the spirit of heaviness is the cause of depression; it can be broken off, and you can be delivered from it.

> ...to console those who mourn in Zion, to give
> them beauty for ashes, the oil of joy for mourning,
> the garment of praise for the spirit of heaviness;
> that they may be called trees of righteousness, the
> planting of the LORD, that He may be glorified.
>
> —ISAIAH 61:3, NKJV

Here Isaiah tells us that the Lord has given us a garment of praise for the spirit of heaviness. Once we've fallen deep into failurism, it's tough to praise to create joy we can have instead of the heaviness and mourning. We must recognize what's going on and that the spirit of failurism is attacking us; otherwise we will never see how to praise our way out.

> The LORD is my strength and my shield; my heart
> trusted in Him, and I am helped; therefore my
> heart greatly rejoices, and with my song I will
> praise Him.
>
> —PSALM 28:7, NKJV

Once we become depressed, it's challenging to find that place where our hearts rejoice with a song of praise. Sadly, once we get to the place where we can't recognize what's happening, we turn to other means to mask the symptoms, usually medication.

I will share a story about a woman we will call Linda. Linda was delivered from depression during one of our miracle and healing services. The Lord already spoke to me before the service and said He wanted to bring deliverance to those attending the service. Deliverance is a different type of healing. I asked those who needed deliverance from particular demonic strongholds or oppressive spirits to come up, and we would pray for them and break off the strongholds or spirits. Linda came up to the altar, not knowing what to expect. She had never attended a miracle healing service before and had been invited by one of our church members. While a little reluctant to come to the altar, she knew she needed deliverance and healing from depression. At that point in the service, I had given instructions and explained to those in attendance what it meant to have oppressive spirits attached to you and that it is a form of healing in our lives to be delivered from those attachments. Linda came to the altar. I prayed for her and walked her through the prayer of repentance and renouncing the spirit of depression. As the Lord broke the yoke of depression, Linda immediately relaxed and began to cry uncontrollably. I continued to pray for her, and she continued to manifest as the glory was ministering and delivering her.

After that service, Linda began to attend our church regularly, and she shared her testimony with me about what God had done that day at the altar. Linda told me how she had battled with depression for years and how she used to be overweight. She worked so hard to lose weight and get healthy, but she was still on medication because she didn't know what else to do. Linda was so down and felt she had no other choice than to take medication. Linda said that when she came to the altar to be delivered and receive healing from depression, as I broke the yoke, she could feel a literal breaking of weight lift off of her and fall to the floor. Then she felt light as a feather, as though she were floating on a lovely cloud. Linda had never experienced anything like that before in her life. She was completely delivered and set free and no longer has to take medication. Today, Linda remains delivered from many other things, and God is using her mightily in His kingdom for His work.

This is only one example of the reality of and truth about the spirit of depression and the spirit of failurism. These oppressive spirits are real, and they're out to destroy your life and to keep you from fulfilling your God-given call, even if that call is being a mom of four giant killers.

CHAPTER 8

OUR APPEARANCE TO OTHERS

IN GENERAL, MOST of us care about how we look to others—not that we're full-on people pleasers, but we care about how we present ourselves because it's an important quality to have. It's important to have self-respect and to care about the impressions we make on others. But when we are battling the spirit of failurism, we take it to another level.

As we are spiraling down through these manifestations, we begin to feel and believe that others look at us as failures—the same way we judge ourselves as failures. In response to that, we become very sensitive and emotional about everything. The emotions can look dramatic, with or without tears, and there are many forms. And of course, when you've gotten to this point with the spirit of failurism still attached to you, you haven't recognized it. You're going to have a whole lot of symptoms, so it's easy to become sensitive and emotional at this level of oppression.

What's sad about this is we genuinely believe that others feel a certain way about us or look at us a certain way, not realizing the whole time that the spirit of failurism is causing us and our emotions to be tossed around. The entire time we're deflecting and judging ourselves, we truly begin to believe that others look at us as failures. So our reactions cause a whole other set of manifestations. As James 1:6 says, we can't accomplish anything or expect anything if we're constantly tossed around to and fro.

We have to know what we believe and whom we believe. If we let our emotions take control and allow our feelings to lead us around, then we continue to fall deeper into failurism and manifest those emotions in ways that are not healthy at all. When I spoke about the spirit of failurism at the beginning of this book, I shared a story about a gentleman named John; one of his key manifestations was his emotions were completely out of control. He was controlling and angry, and he had outbursts of anger. He was all over the place and unstable. One day, he was up, excited, and happy; the next day, he was down and depressed and didn't want to get out of bed. That emotional roller coaster almost ruined his current marriage. When you fall this deep into failurism, the manifestations, symptoms, and spirit of failurism oppress you. Let's look at some of the ways that happens.

First and foremost is confusion. When emotions are tossed around, confusion settles in. We begin feeling unsure, have trouble making decisions, and can't recognize God's true voice. This is also a spirit sent by the enemy. Its purpose is to bring confusion to believers so they will continue to be tossed around by every wave. If you're constantly unsure and feeling confused, it leads to other emotional side effects. It can be very frustrating to feel confused and not understand what's going on when you're oppressed by the spirit of confusion. You're emotional and frustrated and don't know why. It's important to recognize any time any stronghold binds you, whether it's failurism or Jezebel. If you're manifesting the symptoms in your life, you're opening the door for other oppressive spirits to come in and attach.

Your physical actions and reactions can open new doors and welcome in oppressive spirits. Let me share a story about how the spirit of confusion attacked my husband. Through this experience, we realized just how real the spirit of confusion is and that it is sent out, does attack us, and is attached to us if we open the door.

It was a regular Sunday morning, and we were preparing for Sunday service. We were planting a church, so there was a lot of setup and preparation that had to happen before service. My husband was doing what he usually did and making sure everything was set out. The media was ready, and we proceeded with the service; everything went as it usually did. But on that day, the message was not the standard. It was a special message, as we were teaching on the Holy Spirit and baptism of fire. We had seven people baptized in the Holy Spirit, and it was a fantastic day of ministry. But when we got home, my husband started to act very off, short, frustrated, and annoyed for no reason. On that day, we were preparing to teach our next class, a growth track class for new believers and those wanting to become church members, I asked my husband to help me get the papers stapled together for the packets. But since he was acting very off, I told him maybe he should relax for an hour or two and then help me work on the packets later. I printed and got everything ready so that all he needed to do was staple the packets together.

He came into the office and stapled the papers together. After he was done, I stuck some in a big pile and got them ready by putting them in folders for those attending the class. Everything seemed fine, although my husband was still acting very off.

Fast forward a few hours. I was teaching the opening portion of the class, and we were getting ready to start the first video. I went to the back of the church and sat next to my husband while the video was playing. I asked him, "What's up?"

He said, "What do you mean, 'What's up?'"

I said, "You're acting really off, something is wrong, and you need to rebuke it."

He said, "I don't know what's wrong; I just feel off."

I said, "Well, you need to go into the church office and ask God what it is. You need to lay hands on yourself and rebuke it because something is on you."

He left the church, went into the office, and was gone for about fifteen minutes before returning. I asked him, "What was going on? What did you have to remove?"

He said, "I went into the office, sat down, and prayed. I

asked God what was going on and why I felt this way. The Lord told me the spirit of confusion was attacking me and that it had been sent out that morning."

The spirit was sent out to disrupt the morning service and the teaching about the Holy Spirit. When that didn't work, it got angry and latched on to him to disrupt the rest of his day. So my husband laid hands on himself, rebuked and bound the spirit of confusion, and commanded it to leave in the name of Jesus Christ. He immediately felt it lift, the fog was gone, and he could think clearly. But that wasn't the only thing that happened.

After the video was over, I went up to talk about it. Then I handed out the paperwork and study guide that went with the video so everyone could answer the first set of questions. When people looked at their booklets, some said they had chapter three missing or pages four and five were missing. Then others said some of the pages were in the back that were supposed to be in the front, such as chapter two in the back and chapter six in the front. My husband stapled everything together incorrectly. He was so confused by the spirit of confusion that he couldn't even staple together the booklet in order! This is serious business, y'all. The spirit of confusion will destroy full days and cause you not to accomplish anything. I saw it with my own eyes. The devil jumps on the opportunity to make you feel unsure and confused, leading to even more frustration.

PRAYER FOR
DELIVERANCE FROM THE SPIRIT OF CONFUSION

Lay hands on yourself and repeat this prayer:

> *I rebuke and bind the spirit of confusion. I command you to take your hands off of me in the name of Jesus Christ. Amen.*

Lay hands on your forehead and pray:

> *I release a spirit of clarity and command fogginess to go in the name of Jesus Christ. Amen.*

CHAPTER 9

IT'S GOING TO BLOW

As we battle, our emotions and frustration set in. Then anger begins to rise, and we usually have no idea where it came from or began. When we believe it came from a particular person or situation, that's usually just a symptom and not related. It's a side effect and a continued manifestation of the spirit of failurism. Anger is inevitable once you get to a place where you feel so low about yourself. The anger brews inside and will make its way out, depending on your deliverance stage.

If you've been battling with the demon of failurism for twenty years, you will have already shown symptoms of anger. If it's a recent attack, hopefully you will recognize anger in your life before it builds up inside and manifests in your life, or you release it to others in a destructive way. The anger that comes from failurism is deadly. It leads to mass shootings, abuse in the home, abuse of children, and the list goes on and on. Once you live a life being tossed to and fro by your emotions and living in frustration to the point of anger, you will live a life lashing out at others. By the time you get to anger, you've already walked through a process of all previous manifestations and attachments. The buildup becomes tremendous, and you are so led by your emotions, frustrations, and anger that it gets to the point of being life destroying.

The demon of failurism must be broken off your life so that you don't make it to this stage in the process of oppression. But if you are at this point or have surpassed this point, know there's hope for you. There's deliverance and freedom in this book through the power of the Holy Spirit and the blood of Jesus Christ.

If you've made it this far in the book, it's probably hard for you to believe that all these manifestations are connected to one demonic stronghold, the spirit of failurism. Unfortunately, this isn't the end of the list; there's more. Fortunately, we have a mighty God who cares and has a wonderful plan. If you're reading this book, He's going to help you learn not just to break but also to conquer the spirit of failurism in your life.

CHAPTER 10

HIGH EXPECTATIONS

THERE'S THIS FANTASTIC book called *The Bait of Satan* by John Bevere. I recommend reading it if you have not already. It will change your life forever! After anger, the next manifestation is one that John Bevere talks about in chapters one and two of his book: setting expectations of ourselves too high.

Usually, that translates into having too high of expectations of others. What we expect out of ourselves, we also expect out of others, and we treat them accordingly. If you're already walking in unstable emotions such as confusion, anger, and frustration, that will definitely be portrayed to those not meeting your expectations. We don't even know we're doing it most of the time. We have no idea that we have set such high expectations for ourselves that we can't meet, and we end up placing them on others. Once you've gotten this far into failurism, you are definitely to the point you are expecting too much out of yourself. By now, you're doing everything by works of the flesh and not by the Spirit. There will always be limits to the works of the flesh. Not everything is not possible with the flesh, and because of that, we judge what we accomplish through the works of the flesh. Then we deflect that onto others if their "works of the flesh" are not meeting our expectations.

Here's a quote from *The Bait of Satan*:

> If I have expectations about certain persons, those people can let me down. They will disappoint me to the degree that they fall short of my expectations. But if I have no expectations about someone, anything given is a blessing and not something owed. We set ourselves up for offense when we require certain behaviors from those with whom we have relationships. The more we expect, the greater the potential offense.[1]

In that chapter of the book, Bevere is talking about how we set up different levels of expectation according to who people are in our lives: pastor, spouse, children, etc. The reality is that we also set too high expectations on ourselves, especially if we're walking in the spirit of failurism. No matter how well we do, we can never get that feeling we've measured up, and we place that on others too. That leaves room for the existing anger and frustration to bubble up to the surface. It causes lashing out at others who don't meet our expectations, which comes out as offense in our lives. We will be offended by everyone who doesn't meet our expectations because we constantly offend ourselves for not meeting certain expectations. You can see now that this is a vicious cycle going deeper into the manifestations and symptoms of the stronghold of failurism.

CHAPTER 11

TOSSED ABOUT

THERE WAS A family who regularly attended our church. The wife was very faithful, and we will call her Jennifer. She frequently attended with her four children and went to all the groups in which her children were involved. Jennifer's husband, whom we will call Brian, did not want anything to do with attending church, and that went on for a couple of years. Then, finally, we began to make progress with him, and he began attending church faithfully. A couple of months went by, and Brian seemed to be getting in the groove of the men's group and participating in events. But he just couldn't break failurism and had no idea he was bound with it.

A couple of things happened that sent Brian into a tailspin. He lost his job, was looking for work, and severe failurism set in. Brian already battled trusting and believing God was real but was finally at a place where he was faithful. However, his mind was so unstable that he could not get firmly planted. What's scary about when you get to this place is you begin to question your belief in God. Failurism causes you to become erratic in your mind and your thoughts.

Brian began to question his belief in God and had gotten to a point where he was literally willing to believe that there was no God due to his mind being so unstable and the attack of failurism on his life. His wife, Jennifer, had come to us and told us that he was having questions and was sounding unstable. He was being tossed around and was constantly going back and forth. Here's the thing: all of us go through times when we struggle and are unsure about what's happening. But this was deeper. Once you get to the point of your mind becoming unstable because of failurism, it can lead to severe unbelief, and you can actually walk entirely away from your relationship with Christ. That is why it is crucial that failurism is broken and defeated in our lives; its goal is to destroy you.

> But when you ask, you must believe and not doubt, because the one who doubts is like a wave of the sea, blown and tossed by the wind. That person should not expect to receive anything from the Lord. Such a person is double-minded and unstable in all they do.
> — JAMES 1: 6–8, NIV

James is clear there has to be a point of *no* return with our walks and relationships with Christ, a place where even during a battle, we trust who God is when we're unsure about our circumstances changing or getting better. But failurism will keep you in a place of being unstable. By the time you have gone this far and deep, the instability will only lead to one thing, which is our next manifestation.

CHAPTER 12

THE WALKOUT

WHAT'S THE WALKOUT? The walkout is when you choose to walk out of your relationship with Jesus because your unstable mind has fallen prey to complete unbelief. It is the next symptom of the spirit of failurism. Unbelief is deadly, and it can be almost impossible to come back if you've gotten this far in the manifestations. Of course, nothing is impossible with God, but it can be difficult to turn an unbelieving mind back.

Brian never turned back, and he did the walkout. He was so unstable and deep into failurism that he couldn't make any committed decisions, which led to total unbelief. He couldn't grasp that God is real.

I believe there's hope for Brian. There's always hope when you recognize and break failurism, and I've seen some progress. I believe that God is slowly working on Brian to bring him back in the relationship with Him. That's why James was adamant about not allowing ourselves to be tossed around and letting it lead to instability, as that leads to unbelief. The devil loves to get you to this place, believing he has won. He also thinks the call and anointing on your life have been destroyed, so then he doesn't have to worry about you bringing anyone else into God's kingdom and following the call.

Even if we struggle with failurism, it's critical to know that the enemy, Satan, wants to destroy any purpose you have on the earth. We must all know and recognize that we have an enemy who is always looking to disrupt, distract, and influence us to forget the big picture. We have an enemy who has been plotting and scheming against us since before we were born to put a wedge between God and us. We were born with a purpose, and God has a beautiful plan for our lives.

Let's read this story from Mark 9:16–25:

> And he asked them, "What are you arguing about with them?" And someone from the crowd answered him, "Teacher, I brought my son to you, for he has a spirit that makes him mute. And whenever it seizes him, it throws him down, and he foams and grinds his teeth and becomes rigid. So I asked your disciples to cast it out, and they were not able." And he answered them, "O faithless generation, how long am I to be with you? How long am I to bear with you? Bring him to me." And they brought the boy to him. And when the spirit saw him, immediately it convulsed the boy, and he fell on the ground and rolled about, foaming at the mouth. And Jesus asked his father,

"How long has this been happening to him?" And he said, "From childhood. And it has often cast him into fire and into water, to destroy him. But if you can do anything, have compassion on us and help us." And Jesus said to him, "'If you can'! All things are possible for one who believes." Immediately the father of the child cried out and said, "I believe; help my unbelief!" And when Jesus saw that a crowd came running together, he rebuked the unclean spirit, saying to it, "You mute and deaf spirit, I command you, come out of him and never enter him again."

This story is amazing, and I love deliverance stories! (Of course, I do, or I wouldn't be writing this book!) It is what we're exactly talking about here. Think about what can be accomplished when you believe. Believing is powerful! Jesus said we would do greater things than He did (John 14:12). Do you know how scary that is for the devil? These verses say it all and what belief can do. It can set the captives free—even ourselves! The devil is trying to stop that. It sounds so simple, but it's not. How many people never walk or follow God's call because their unbelief grew out of the spirit of failurism? The devil hates what an on-fire believer can accomplish on the earth, and this story shows what can be achieved.

There was this lovely family whom we will call the Smith family. They had a heart for the Lord and had spent their lives serving Him. They had raised their children in a Spirit-filled church and were very faithful. Still, one of their children, their son, allowed himself to get involved with information and research, which caused him to become unstable. He began to question whether God was real. And this young man allowed himself to be tossed around by the things he was reading and watching, conspiracy theories, new age, etc. He ultimately, in his instability, completely walked away from God and decided he did not believe in Him. I unfortunately have many, many other similar stories I could tell you. This can happen when you become unstable. It leads to unbelief, and the spirit of failurism promotes that unbelief.

CHAPTER 13

FEAR, FEAR, FEAR

LET'S DIVE A little deeper into the story of the Smith family. As I said earlier, they are a lovely family, and their son had become so unstable because of worldly influence that he walked away from God altogether. While all this was happening, Sam and Lori Smith made the hard decision to ask their son to move out. Their son chose not to serve the Lord and was headed in the wrong direction, and they were put in a position to ask him to leave.

Several years went by, and he moved out of town. He went through a bunch of drama and stress and realized that he really needed his family. He reached out to Sam and Lori to see if there was a possibility of moving back home. After a lot of prayer and consideration, Sam and Lori decided to allow him to move back home. Several months went by, and things seemed to be going OK, other than he was struggling with church attendance. The longer he was there, the more Sam and Lori began to recognize there appeared to be a tremendous amount of oppression within their home. Their atmosphere was not clean and was being destroyed little by little.

After about six months, they approached my husband and me and asked us to anoint their house, pray over it, and cleanse it. While walking through the house, praying, and doing what we do, I recognized and discerned demonic activity in the atmosphere. When we got to specific rooms, we noticed there was a shift. There was a section in their large living room area where they had a dining table, and the entire table was covered with ancient demonic artifacts. Sam and Laurie asked if we could pray over them and break off anything brought in; they knew something was brought in because they could feel that the atmosphere had gotten worse over the last six months.

We prayed over the artifacts, and then I pulled Lori aside as my husband and Sam were still looking at the artifacts. I asked her why those artifacts were in their home when they knew demonic attachments were connected with them. Immediately she began to get teary eyed, and I immediately discerned in the spirit that there was a spirit of fear attached to her. I said, "You're afraid to say something to your son because he had to leave home once, and you don't want him to need to go again."

She said, "Yes, I'm terrified of losing my son."

I explained to her that she was possibly battling the spirit of failurism, causing her to have fear.

She asked, "What is failurism?"

I explained the spirit of failurism, told her I was writing this book, and talked about everything I'm sharing with you.

She broke down and cried and said, "That's exactly it. That's exactly how I feel."

I told her that fear is a manifestation when the spirit of failurism attaches to you. So I began to walk her through why the spirit of failurism would have an open door to attach itself to her. As I talked her through it, Lori felt she failed her son when he was younger. Lori believed she should have been able to stop him from walking away from God, and she felt like a failure. Because she felt like a failure, she was too afraid to say anything about the demonic artifacts in her home, as she didn't want to fail her son again. I explained to her the spirit of failurism has many manifestations, but one of them is the spirit of fear.

I said, "Your fear is based on failurism, not based on God convicting you. We need to break that off so that you can clearly see what should and should not be happening in your home, and you must trust that God loves your son more than you do and has a wonderful plan." I then explained to Lori that when you walk into failurism, you open the door to many manifestations. Once you open the door to fear, you have that spirit attached to you, clearing up the devil's use of fear through failurism to keep you from doing anything that would promote growth, cleansing, or purity. I said, "Failure and fear work together to keep your son bound. And he's bound because he won't do anything to help unbind him because of fear and failurism."

Lori said, "Why have I never heard about this before?

I've been dealing with these symptoms of manifestations for years, and the whole time it was the demon of failurism attacking me." Lori's mind was blown, and she was ready to pray to break off the demon of failurism and the fear that had been haunting her for six months, keeping her from making any progress with her son.

Take this story and look back at all the other manifestations we've already discussed. You can now put pieces of the puzzle together and see how easy it is for the spirit of failurism to open the door to other demonic activity and attachments. While the spirit of fear promotes all fear, it's commonly another door that's been opened. Fear is a by-product of the other door that's been opened.

Second Timothy 1:7 says, "For God has not given us a spirit of fear, but of power and of love and of a sound mind" (NKJV). God has not given us a life of bondage, and this fear is not from Him. He has given us power, love, and a sound mind.

PRAYER FOR
DELIVERANCE FROM THE SPIRIT OF FEAR

Lay hands on yourself and repeat these prayers:

Repent (eyes open):

> *Dear heavenly Father, I repent right now for walking in the spirit of fear; please forgive me in the name of Jesus Christ.*

Renounce (eyes open):

> *I renounce the spirit of fear. I break all contracts previously made with this demon in the name of Jesus Christ of Nazareth.*

Break the yoke (lay hands on yourself with eyes open):

> *I break the yoke of the spirit of fear off my life in the name of Jesus Christ. I command it to leave and never to return, I pull fear up by the root, and I cast it to the ground to come to nothing in the name of Jesus Christ. I release faith to fill that place where fear once was in my life in the name of Jesus Christ. Amen.*

CHAPTER 14

LASHING OUT

L ET'S GO BACK to John's story from the beginning of the book. He was battling a severe case of failurism. As I said, he became very strict and rigid, and everything had to be perfect in its place. He constantly judged everyone and everything around him by how he felt about himself. Once you're that deep into failurism, you will likely walk through all these manifestations in some form. And by this time, you are lashing out at everyone around you. The reality is that you are upset with yourself, but you take it out on others, not realizing you're lashing out. You believe you have every right to do what you're doing and think how you're thinking. Still, the entire reason you are lashing out at those around you, especially your immediate family members, is because you're head deep in the manifestations of the spirit of failurism.

When you are this far into the spirit of failurism, you have most likely hurt a lot of people, as well as ruined or broken a lot of relationships. Those close to or affected by you don't understand the root of your problem; it's not how you are but rather that you need deliverance.

One of the previous manifestations is the anger held inside. By now, it's making its way out, and this is where the lashing out comes from. What's sad is people can spend their entire lives lashing out, believing their feelings behind the anger, and creating bad habits and patterns in their thought processes.

I hope you're tracking with me. Jennifer thought the way she acted and reacted was normal and that the way she was receiving information from others gave her a reason to act the way that she did. She felt the other person was at fault for annoying or frustrating her, and her response was normal and deserved. In reality, Jennifer was lashing out the entire time and didn't know it. She truly believed that she was normal, and because Jennifer had lashed out for so long, she was deceived. I lovingly told Jennifer I would start holding her accountable when she lashed out. After that point, anytime we were planning an event or working together, when she lashed out, I immediately said, "You're doing it."

She said, "I am?"

I said, "Yes, you're being angry and impatient for absolutely no reason. Do you not recognize how you sound and how you look?"

Jennifer said, "This is how I've always been."

As you see, it's easy to be deceived and walk in all these manifestations of failurism. You don't even realize the patterns that allow the stronghold of failurism to rise above anything and everything in your life, especially God. I hope this is truly opening your eyes to see how easy it is for us to live our lives based on the manifestations and side effects of the spirit of failurism.

> A hot-tempered man stirs up strife, but he who is
> slow to anger quiets contention.
>   —PROVERBS 15:18

God is not pleased when you lash out. When you don't recognize what you are doing is full of anger that made its way to the surface, you cause strife wherever you go. Then people want to avoid you because you're constantly offending them with your lashing out. It's essential to get to the root of a problem and break the spirit of failurism. It will help you to slowly unravel all these patterns that you've created so that you can see and think clearly, and grow and flourish in every area of your Christian walk, your life, and your relationships.

CHAPTER 15

FALSE SORROW

FALSE SORROW IS the last manifestation I will discuss with you in this book. Aside from failurism itself, it is the biggest issue. By the time you've made your way down through all these manifestations, you will undoubtedly be living and walking in the spirit of false sorrow. What is false sorrow? It is self-abuse; it is fear—false evidence appearing real. When you base your decisions on the fear of others' rejection, you feel flawed or sorrowful for something that isn't real, and even if it becomes real, you're still not guilty. False sorrow is when the devil throws a heavy blanket of sorrow on you that doesn't belong. It's false; it's not yours to carry. Walking in the spirit of false sorrow, you will live a completely different life than you would if you were set free from this stronghold that has come in through the door of failurism.

I said that false sorrow is self-abuse. When dealing with other people, they will blame you and cause you to feel responsible for their woes. They will make you feel responsible for everything going wrong in their lives. They will manipulate you into believing somehow it's your fault.

It becomes self-abuse when you believe the lies. You think that somehow you're responsible, and then you begin to beat yourself up with false sorrow that doesn't belong to you. It's been placed on you by demonic activity through lying spirits. This is huge! The spirit of failurism opens the door for false sorrow, making it easy for you to walk in it. You're so afraid of rejection by the other person that you allow yourself to be abused and manipulated.

Let me share a story of someone bound by false sorrow who came through the spirit of failurism. There was a woman who was in a very turbulent marriage. We will call her Amy. By the time she sought help, Amy was very broken and beaten down. She had been married for eleven years, but she knew something needed to change in her marriage. Amy didn't know what, but she couldn't live in it anymore. Her husband had had several affairs during their relationship, and even though God gave her many checks in her spirit that something was wrong, Amy struggled to believe that it could change. She had allowed herself to be manipulated and knew she was being lied to but did nothing. Her husband constantly said he wouldn't do it again and placed the responsibility on her. That made Amy feel as if she would destroy their marriage if she did anything about it because he had promised not to do it again.

Ever since she was a teenager, she had battled with her weight, so she had very low self-esteem. Because of that, Amy believed somehow it was her fault that her husband had affairs. She believed he would stay faithful if she looked better and was a better wife. And because of this thought process, she lived in failurism on a large scale—so large that false sorrow had taken over her life. In my first session with her, I immediately felt the spirit of false sorrow like a blanket over her.

At that time, she was not ready to receive or understand what was causing the false sorrow. I gave Amy counsel on what to do next in her marriage, and she began to work on it. When she came back for her next session, I asked Amy how things were going and how the changes she was supposed to be working on were going. Amy admitted she hadn't followed through with all the changes because her husband made her feel guilty for standing up to him. She finally decided to do what was right for her and her children.

I explained to Amy that she needed to agree to follow through with everything I told her, the steps she needed to take, and that they would come before her healing for her relationship with Christ and the protection of her children. That counseling would do no good if she weren't following through on the things she needed to do to begin the work of healing. If there was going to be any chance of her marriage being restored, Amy needed to trust what I was telling her to do. She did not understand false sorrow, but I could see it all over her. As Amy explained how he made her feel guilty for every decision made, she went deeper into the pit of manifesting false sorrow from failurism. She truly believed that her husband's affairs were because she was a failure as a wife. Therefore he easily manipulated her, which quickly made the spirit of false sorrow attached to her.

I explained to Amy what he was doing because she didn't even see that she was being manipulated and walking in false sorrow. I told Amy that false sorrow causes you to feel you're at fault for something you're not responsible for. You can love your spouse or love another person, but you are not responsible for that person having the right relationship with Christ and choosing to serve Him. You cannot make them either not walk in a sinful lifestyle or choose a sinful lifestyle. I explained to her that he was making her feel as though she were responsible for his happiness, and she owed it to him to believe what he was saying when he said he wouldn't cheat anymore.

I asked her how many times he promised he wouldn't do it again, and she said, "Three times." I explained to her that she did not owe him her trust. He broke her trust many years before, and that false sorrow oppresses her. I offered to walk her through removing the spirit of false sorrow and explained deliverance. She agreed, and I walked her through breaking the yoke—although this was not the end of the story because failurism can run so deep. Unless you're taught the wrong thought process and what it looks like so that you can be set free, you cannot break free from the manifestations that oppress you.

I hoped that breaking the yoke would give her enough clarity to see what her husband was doing and that she was being kept in bondage. Unfortunately, as the weeks went on, Amy only partially listened to the counsel on what needed to happen with her marriage. Her husband continued to manipulate her, and false sorrow oppressed her as she gave into fear—false evidence appearing real. What was the evidence? Amy's husband continued to produce evidence that was false so that he could continue manipulating her. He made her feel she was accountable for his feelings and rights in the relationship, although he lived in sin. Sadly Amy didn't follow through with the counsel I gave her. Undoubtedly it would've been hard at first to walk through, but ultimately it would have brought healing and either mended the relationship or helped Amy figure out who she was in the Lord, separate from her husband. Anytime she tried to make a decision or even move forward with wise counsel, he would make her feel terribly guilty for even considering following through on what she was told she needed to do.

Amy now knew false sorrow was a true spirit and could recognize she was walking in it, but she couldn't find the strength to rebuke, bind, and take authority over it. She continued to fall right into it. Fast forward six months and Amy chose to let her husband talk her into fixing their marriage his way. I continued to watch him manipulate her as the spirit of all sorrow consumed her to the point where she believed everything he was saying. She knew he usually did not tell the truth, but she felt like such a failure and had so much false sorrow that she continued to blame herself. She thought he was right somehow and she just needed to give in. But this could not heal their marriage because he would have no reason to change or stop his sinful behavior. Six months later, with a broken heart, I had to sit down with Amy and tell her that her husband was still having an affair; this time, it was with two other women simultaneously. I had to walk her through the deliverance of false sorrow once again. She then could see how it had taken over her life and how she believed the lies of the enemy. It would not fix her marriage; it would destroy her marriage. She would never grow or change or be set free if she continued to listen to the lies of failurism and false sorrow.

So how did her story end? Amy ended up being set free from failurism and false sorrow. Amy recognized the value of who she was in Christ and that she did not need to live in that kind of marriage. She was set free. It has been a long, painful road for her to break out of those mindsets and patterns, but she is now a strong woman in Christ who knows who she is and embraces the pain that comes with walking in freedom. I hope this story has helped you to understand how easily we can walk in false sorrow and never become who God has called us to be because of failurism and the manifestations that come with it. Imagine the life Amy would be living if she had continued to be bound in failurism and false sorrow. Amy would be in an unhealthy marriage and not know who she is in Christ. That would also hinder her husband from becoming free and facing his own sin. That is why the devil tries so hard to keep people bound in the stronghold of failurism—to destroy their lives so they don't become who they were born to be.

Let's consider the life of Paul. He had spent all his time fighting against the ministry of the gospel. He killed Christians and was devoted to seeing them pay for spreading the gospel. Once he had his Damascus Road awakening and realized he was actually working against the God of the universe, whom he loved dearly, he could have beaten himself up, allowed failurism to take over, and sat in false sorrow. Yes, he had a reason to repent and things to feel sorry for, but there comes a point when we must receive forgiveness from the Lord Jesus and walk in freedom. Otherwise the devil will bring in failurism and cause you to feel you have no right participating in the call of God. Aren't you thankful Paul did not fall for the spirit of failurism? He repented and felt sorrowful, but then he got up, shook himself off, and began to run with a fire that no one could contain. He ended up writing thirteen books in the New Testament. If failurism had had its way, it would have attached to Paul, and Paul would have never become the mighty apostle that he became. How different it would be without the books in the Bible that he wrote and the testimony of his life. This is why it's so important to defeat and break failurism off of your life once and for all.

In the next few chapters, we're going to answer the question, How can we defeat failurism? We will talk about spiritual and practical ways to break and defeat failurism in your life. You will learn how Jesus alone is your righteousness. Through Him, we are made right and do not have to live in failurism.

CHAPTER 16

THE SPIRIT OF AIMLESSNESS

BREAKING THE SPIRIT of aimlessness is one of the biggest keys to being set free from the spirit of failurism. This demon's primary goal is to keep us from making contact with anything of value or power. First Corinthians 9:26 says we are to run with a goal in mind, "so I do not run aimlessly; I do not box as one beating the air."

Failurism's goal is to keep us beating the air, to waste our time so we never accomplish anything for God's kingdom. We beat the air and never make contact with our true value and purpose. Then failurism can get a firm hold on our lives and destinies through aimlessness. The spirit of aimlessness is a perfect partner with failurism if the body of Christ is not intentional about anything.

So what is aimlessness? It means being "without aim or purpose; not having a goal or purpose."[1] Synonyms of *aimless* are *purposeless, goalless, undirected, unfocused, profitless, fruitless,* etc. I think you get the drift.

The body of Christ does not have time to waste walking in the fruit of the spirit of aimlessness. The enemy, through this spirit, would like to keep God's people fruitless, without a plan or focus. His goal is to keep you purposeless so you never fulfill your destiny.

The Lord gave me a times-and-seasons word in 2020 in the midst of the pandemic. During this season, the church had been put on lockdown in many states, and things were shifting quickly. The church had to come up with a plan to reach people differently.

The Lord spoke to me as I was in serious intercession. He said, "The spirit of aimlessness is attacking My body. This spirit is attempting to make My church believe they have been knocked off their horse, and they have not been knocked off their horse. The horse is just headed in a new direction and season. Let My people know the enemy's schemes and bring deliverance."

In reality, this all goes back to Jesus being our righteousness. If we are aimless or think we have been knocked off our horses, we begin to rely on our own works. We start looking for ways to fix or change it using our human thinking and logic. Sometimes that can lead to manipulation because we're trying to gain control. But what we are using is being created from a by-product of our own works brought on by fear of failing. This spirit is so sneaky and deceptive. It promotes all the work we think we are not doing; it promotes what's not working. It makes us feel as if we are failing somehow, so our groveling in human effort continues to grow the spirit of failurism, and its open door is the spirit of aimlessness.

So what happened through the revelation of a demon coming against God's people during the pandemic? People felt they had lost their footing, fallen off their horses. They had no idea what to do, so they freaked out or panicked because they saw their ministries going down the toilet and being flushed away. Some of them tried to force their way forward doing what they had always done, feeding the feeling of being aimless or failing, in order to remain in their comfort zones by trying to live in the past. That led to people assuming all these things were coming against them, when the whole time, God was and is using the pandemic to move His body into new seasons to prepare us to bring in the end-time harvest.

Another result of God's people feeling aimless during this season was that they either quit or wanted to quit because they had become so reliant on man and money, and they saw everything crumbling. Both reactions—forcing the way forward doing the same old thing or quitting—catered to being aimless and feeling like a failure. But the entire time, God had a different plan. But the spirit of aimlessness was sent to disrupt what the body of Christ had thought to be true. What was that? God has never changed, nothing surprises Him, and *all things work for His glory and our good.*

Therefore, God had a plan, and He used and is using it all to see His plan come to pass on the earth. Why? Because He has already won. Yep, Jesus won on the cross! Don't let aimlessness take root, because the enemy will take that and make way for failurism to continue to steal the truth of who you are and who God is in you. When you don't let aimlessness take root, you will be intentional about your walk and not beat the air or wander around on the earth like a lost puppy who has no purpose. We are all born in season, which means we're chosen from the womb for such a time as this. You are supposed to be here. Your life is not purposeless or without value. Once you truly know this, the spirit of aimlessness will lose its grip and power to partner with or open a door for the spirit of failurism to walk in and become a stronghold.

PRAYER

Dear heavenly Father, I lift every person reading this whom the spirit of aimlessness has attacked. I bind the spirit of aimlessness. I command that demon to take its hands off every person reading this in the name of Jesus Christ. We cast it to the ground to come to nothing. I bind and rebuke the orphan spirit. I command the demon of the orphan to come off of the body of Christ. I command that demon to take its hands off every person battling this now in the name of Jesus Christ of Nazareth. I release purpose. I release the Holy Ghost's purpose. I release Holy Ghost fire and Holy Ghost vision over everyone battling and being attacked with the spirit of aimlessness. And Lord, I release Your glory and Your kingdom to manifest in their lives, and I ask that You would clear away the confusion. Clear away the wondering and the questioning. And I ask that You would release a clarity, Lord, and the fog would lift. I speak that. I pray that right now over every person reading this, in the name of Jesus Christ of Nazareth. Amen!

PART II

JESUS ALONE IS OUR RIGHTEOUSNESS— DEFEATING FAILURISM SPIRITUALLY

CHAPTER 17

WORD CURSES

THE SPIRIT OF failurism and word curses go hand in hand; they work together in unison. The reality is there are many demonic strongholds that are sent out against people through word curses. I have personally experienced the partnership of word curses and the spirit of failurism.

What is a word curse? A word curse is anything spoken out loud into the atmosphere that is contrary to God's will, God's plan, and what God says about you. A word curse is anything that promotes any plan, thought process, or emotion that God has not ordained for you or said about you, your future, and your call—anything that's not true about who you are, who God says you are, or what's true in your heart.

How is this possible? When the words spoken about us or over us do not reflect or align with what God says about us, the enemy grabs onto those words, and they get carried away by demons to be put to work. Demons are assigned to see those word curses—if we do not recognize them as word curses so they can be canceled. Those curses can attach to us, affect our lives, infiltrate our thinking, and even penetrate our souls.

How do Satan and his friends have authority to carry out this work?

> And you He made alive, who were dead in trespasses and sins, in which you once walked according to the course of this world, according to the prince of the power of the air, the spirit who now works in the sons of disobedience, among whom also we all once conducted ourselves in the lusts of our flesh, fulfilling the desires of the flesh and of the mind, and were by nature children of wrath, just as the others.
>
> —EPHESIANS 2:1–3, NKJV

Satan is the God of this world. He's the prince of the power of the air in the earthly realm. That means he has the ability to put power behind word curses sent out through the air as they are spoken by humans. He has the authority to do that in the earthly realm.

> Then war broke out in heaven. Michael and his angels fought against the dragon, and the dragon and his angels fought, but they did not prevail, nor was there a place for them in heaven any longer. The great dragon was cast out, that ancient serpent called the Devil and Satan, who deceives the whole world. He was cast down to

the earth, and his angels were cast down with him.

—REVELATION 12:7–9, MEV

You ask, How can words be so powerful? How can the devil possibly have this much power? Let's see what the apostle Paul had to say about spoken words.

Let no corrupt word proceed out of your mouth, but what is good for necessary edification, that it may impart grace to the hearers. And do not grieve the Holy Spirit of God, by whom you were sealed for the day of redemption. Let all bitterness, wrath, anger, clamor, and evil speaking be put away from you, with all malice. And be kind to one another, tenderhearted, forgiving one another, even as God in Christ forgave you.

—EPHESIANS 4:29–32, NKJV

The apostle Paul made it very clear that what we speak matters, the spoken word matters. Prophets prophesy the spoken word out loud and evangelists preach the gospel out loud with their voices, but there's also a negative side to what we speak, which Paul clearly addressed in these verses. If there were no power behind the spoken word, then speaking curses and other negative things would not be addressed in the Bible as something to avoid.

Now back to the story I alluded to at the beginning of

the chapter. Around the time I was just about finished writing this book, I began to feel a heavy weight. I was very weighed down with a lot of thoughts that I knew were not of the Lord. I rebuked them and cast off several things, but the heavy weight and the feeling that something was just off would not leave. I felt off for a couple of days. I left to go pray and sit at a prayer mountain where I often go.

I was praying in the spirit on the way there. The Lord spoke to me and said, "Word curses. You need to break word curses. Word curses have been sent out against you, and the spirit of failurism has latched on to them. You need to cancel them and bind their power so what is coming against you can be removed." I walked myself through canceling and binding the power and effects of any and all word curses sent out against me. Boom! The weight lifted and I was delivered. I have personal knowledge that word curses and failurism work hand in hand.

I have a staff member who was also attacked through the partnership of word curses and the spirit of failurism. The staff member went to an event and was truly blessed by God. The testimony of everything that the Lord did through the revival he attended was beautiful. But there were some very prideful and evidently religious people connected with our ministry who had negative things to say about those who were truly blessed at this revival and had testimonies; basically their testimonies were being degraded.

The truth about how these prideful religious people really felt was very hurtful to the staff member. Although his testimony was great and beautiful, the negative words spoken turned into word curses, and this staff member began to feel very weighed down and as if his testimony didn't matter or have value. The staff member came to me for help and deliverance from how he was feeling about the situation. I knew immediately that the word curses had produced an open door for the spirit of failurism to attach to him. As soon as I said it, he immediately knew that that's what it was. We canceled word curses and their power and bound the spirit of failurism, and immediately everything lifted.

Word curses are very real, and they seem to have a beautiful partnership with the spirit of failurism. It's important the people of God recognize this partnership so they know how to handle it when these manifestations come.

PRAYER FOR

PROTECTION FROM WORD CURSES

Here's the prayer I recommend you pray regularly over yourself as a protection from word curses and the power behind them:

> *I cancel every demonic word curse spoken over me, anything spoken over me that is not true of who God says I am, not true of who I know I am, and not true of God's plan for me. I bind the power behind those words spoken over me that are not true, and I bind the effects and the manifestations of any word curses spoken, in the name of Jesus Christ.*

CHAPTER 18

REPENT OF UNBELIEF

WHOA, WAIT A minute! Repent? Why? What exactly is unbelief?

According to *Merriam-Webster*, *unbelief* means "incredulity or skepticism especially in matters of religious faith."[1] *Strong's* defines the Greek word for *unbelief* as "faithlessness, i.e. (negatively) disbelief (lack of Christian faith), or (positively) unfaithfulness (disobedience)."[2] Wow! Unbelief is a huge problem, and it must go if we are to defeat failurism.

Consider the story of George. He's living life, and everything is just going terrible. He feels as if he is at the bottom of a pit and has come to a realization that his life needs Christ. George is all excited and ready for a new life. He chooses to accept Christ into his heart and life and goes forward in victory. He jumps all in, swimming in the glory and swimming in salvation. George goes to church on Sundays, maybe Wednesdays, but isn't changing anything in his life. The next thing you know, he's just living life and continuing to think and live the same way. When he is faced with some struggles and attacks, it all goes downhill. Now he's depressed and living a powerless Christian life. George decides not to get over his past failures and struggles to move forward. He begins to live a life that looks as though he truly doesn't believe in the salvation that he received and the power and freedom in it.

Oh, of course, George still calls himself a Christian and still faithfully shows up on Sundays with a smile on his face, lifting his hands during worship. Yet deep inside he denies the power behind the salvation he received. It is no longer working in his life because he has fallen into unbelief and doesn't even know. He has turned his back on the salvation given to him as a free gift. George believes that because he's doing all the right things and saved, he must accept that he will still have the same thought patterns and ways of making decisions. And that is who he is.

> He has delivered us from the domain of darkness and transferred us to the kingdom of his beloved Son, in whom we have redemption, the forgiveness of sins.
>
> —COLOSSIANS 1:13–14

This verse is powerful! Here Paul is stating that God has delivered us from the domain of darkness and transferred us to the kingdom of His Son. But what happens, as we saw from the example of George, is people receive Christ but live powerless lives. That happens when we stop believing in the power of the cross and the salvation we received.

When that happens, we begin a pattern of unbelief. We don't even know we're walking in unbelief. We're basically saying the power of salvation is not strong enough to transfer us from darkness to light. Hence, we continue to live in a place of darkness and defeat. Our unbelief causes us to believe that salvation is not strong enough to overcome our past failures, so we continue to live in them and walk in them. We must repent for our unbelief, as repentance is foundational to being spiritually delivered from the spirit of failurism and defeating it in our lives.

We must repent for not living and walking in the power of the cross, and for allowing the cross to lose its value in our lives. When we know who Christ is and what He's done for us, and still choose to believe nothing can change and we are just failures, we are telling Jesus that His shed blood on the cross was not enough! That is extremely self-centered! You might think, "Wow, that's harsh!" Yes, it is—because we must all realize the importance of repenting when we are walking in unbelief. We must know how selfish it is and how it removes the power of the cross and all Jesus did in our lives. God always starts with repentance.

When I was preparing this study and was teaching it to our church, the Lord told me they needed to repent for their unbelief. I thought, "Wow, that's extreme." I asked God, "Why?"

He said, "They stopped believing in My saving power, all that I've done for them. They need to repent for it, and that repentance for unbelief is the start of defeating failurism."

The reality is that without salvation, our faith in Christ, and what He's done for us on the cross, there is nothing that is the beginning of everything. There is nothing to build upon. That is why repentance for unbelief is so important. We must believe in the power of the cross to move forward in victory and defeat failurism.

> And without faith it is impossible to please him, for whoever would draw near to God must believe that he exists and that he rewards those who seek him.
>
> —HEBREWS 11:6

We must believe and have faith, and we must have faith in the salvation we have received. If we live our whole lives in unbelief and doubt, it makes it hard for God to release the rewards we receive when we follow Him wholeheartedly and the manifestations that come from those blessings. When the spirit of failurism tries to attach to us, it would not be able to oppress us so quickly if we didn't walk in unbelief. But failurism's goal is to keep you stuck so you never move forward. When that happens, your salvation is worthless because you never actually live the life that Christ died for you to have.

PRAYER OF
REPENTANCE FOR WALKING IN UNBELIEF

Let's repent for unbelief and renew our hearts in Christ before we move on to the next chapter. Lay hands on yourself and repeat this prayer:

> *Dear heavenly Father, I repent for walking in unbelief. Please forgive me for giving in to myself and believing the enemy's lies that Your cross has no value or power. I give my life back to You, and I ask You to fill my heart again with all You are and the salvation I originally received. I ask for the power of the cross to reside in me in the name of Jesus Christ. Amen!*

CHAPTER 19

WALK IN AUTHORITY

W E MUST REBUKE and bind the spirit of failurism in our lives and command it go! We can walk ourselves through self-deliverance anytime on a daily basis. When we feel the effects of failurism's manifestations, we can take authority over it. So how do we take command of it? What does it mean to rebuke and bind?

The *King James Dictionary* says *rebuke* means "to reprimand; strongly warn; restrain."[1] In Matthew, Jesus rebuked the wind, and it obeyed:

> And he said to them, "Why are you afraid, O you of little faith?" Then he rose and rebuked the winds and the sea, and there was a great calm.
> —MATTHEW 8:26

Jesus took authority over the wind and the sea. We have that same authority to rebuke anything the enemy brings against us. We must take authority. Jesus said in John that we would do the works He has done and even greater works.

Truly, truly, I say to you, whoever believes in me will also do the works that I do; and greater works than these will he do, because I am going to the Father. Whatever you ask in my name, this I will do, that the Father may be glorified in the Son. If you ask me anything in my name, I will do it.

—JOHN 14:12–14

Boom! Jesus Himself has given us authority. He also said in Luke that He had given us authority:

The 70 disciples came back very happy. They said, "Lord, even demons obey us when we use the power and authority of your name!"

Jesus said to them, "I watched Satan fall from heaven like lightning. I have given you the authority to trample snakes and scorpions and to destroy the enemy's power. Nothing will hurt you."

—LUKE 10:17–19, GW

We have power and authority through the power of the Holy Spirit, just like the seventy disciples sent out. But most of the time, we don't realize our authority, so we don't walk in it. We allow ourselves to be constantly beaten up by the enemy and his schemes, but in the name of Jesus Christ, we have power and authority, and we need to rise up and use it.

What does *bind* mean?

> I will give you the keys of the kingdom of heaven,
> and whatever you bind on earth shall be bound
> in heaven, and whatever you loose on earth shall
> be loosed in heaven.
>
> —MATTHEW 16:19

If what is coming against us is not of God and not of heaven, we definitely have the authority to bind it, take control, and loose what heaven says about us.

What does God say about us?

> What then shall we say to these things? If God
> is for us, who can be against us? He who did
> not spare his own Son but gave him up for us
> all, how will he not also with him graciously
> give us all things? Who shall bring any charge
> against God's elect? It is God who justifies. Who
> is to condemn? Christ Jesus is the one who died—
> more than that, who was raised—who is at the
> right hand of God, who indeed is interceding for
> us. Who shall separate us from the love of Christ?
> Shall tribulation, or distress, or persecution, or
> famine, or nakedness, or danger, or sword? As
> it is written, "For your sake we are being killed
> all the day long; we are regarded as sheep to be
> slaughtered." No, in all these things we are more
> than conquerors through him who loved us. For

I am sure that neither death nor life, nor angels
nor rulers, nor things present nor things to come,
nor powers, nor height nor depth, nor anything
else in all creation, will be able to separate us
from the love of God in Christ Jesus our Lord.
—ROMANS 8:31–39

That is what we declare and loose over our lives!

One thing that tries to keep us from walking in our authority is the spirit of intimidation. Intimidation is a killer. It will squash the Holy Spirit working through you. Most of the time when we're intimidated, we don't know it. We make our problems or the enemy's attacks out to be bigger and more powerful than they are, but God needs us to walk in authority and not fall prey to intimidation. If we're intimidated, we will not even fight for ourselves, and we will dive deeper into the spirit of failurism. When we take authority, things may not change overnight, but over time the enemy will get the drift that it's not going to work, and he will move on.

First Peter 5:8 says, "Be sober-minded; be watchful. Your adversary the devil prowls around like a roaring lion, seeking someone to devour." There's a breaking point in any area of our lives when we're trying to gain victory, but once we cross over the line, we will have the victory. Even if failurism shows up later, it won't be able to impact us the way it has in the past. The devil will always be prowling around and most likely will try to get at you differently. As a Christian, that is inevitable, but as you stand in authority against the spirit of failurism, it will eventually back off.

As I said earlier, I was attacked by the spirit of failurism on a massive scale. One final attack that the enemy tried to bring against me was to keep me from writing this book, but it left once I crossed over and took full authority. I took its power; it will still try to creep in, but it has no effect.

Luke 9:1–2 says, "And he called the twelve together and gave them power and authority over all demons and to cure diseases, and he sent them out to proclaim the kingdom of God and to heal." Jesus has made it very clear we have authority, and He has given it to us. We must understand it is not just to serve others and help others; it's also for our own self-deliverance and our own walks of faith. We must draw a line in the sand, stay behind the line, and stand firm.

There was a time in my life when I was under severe attack as a new Christian. The first few years of my salvation, the enemy fought hard to get me to go back to my old life and turn from the knowledge of the power of the cross and the power that I felt and experienced in the name of Jesus Christ during my radical salvation and deliverance. Satan attacked me on a massive scale with fear and night terrors those first few years. His goal was to wear me down so I would quit going forward and running with the passion of the Lord, the passion I had been running with since the day I was radically saved. Satan tried everything to suck the life out of me with the spirit of fear.

Finally, one night at 3:00 a.m., I had had enough. I was so done with the attacks and my sleep being interrupted every single night that I got up, went into my bathroom, and closed the door so that I would not wake up my husband. I stood there, firmly stuck my finger out at the devil, and said, "Devil, I'm done with you. Spirit of fear, I'm done with you. You will not mess with me in the night anymore. I dare you to come and face me in person! You would not face me because you're a coward. Come on, devil, we're going to duke it out because it ends tonight. I rebuke and bind you, and I command you to leave this house and never to return, and if you show up tomorrow night when I'm trying to sleep, I will take you out! Now I'm going back to bed, and you just need to leave and leave me alone because it will not work. I am saved, delivered, and set free, and I will never turn back. Your game is done, in Jesus' name!"

After that night, I was never attacked in my sleep again, but I was tortured for three years before I took authority. Why did I let it go on so long? The reason was that although we were at a Spirit-filled church, I hadn't learned about deliverance ministry, defeating demons, and the power of binding and rebuking. All I had was the first experience right before I was radically saved. I was being attacked by demons and rebuked them in the name of Jesus Christ of

Nazareth, and they left. Not too long after that, I was radically saved, and demons fled my body screaming. I had to take myself back to that day and remind myself of the authority and the power in the name of Jesus Christ. After three years of torture and finally realizing I had the power of the Holy Spirit and Jesus Christ on my side, I knew that from that day forward I didn't have to accept anything the devil threw at me. I had the authority to rebuke and bind it by the power of the Holy Spirit.

It's also imperative as you learn to take authority and walk in authority that you stop loosing the negative things you think about your life or that you feel about yourself. You have to know that Satan will attach to anything and try to squeeze into any open door. You need to bind and rebuke, and then you need to loose the opposite. Don't keep releasing the same negativity: "I'm just a failure. I'm just a sinner. I'm always going to walk in sin. I've tried walking in the spirit, but I just can't do it. I keep failing. I guess I just can't hear God. God doesn't speak to me anymore. I have failed too many times, so He doesn't love me anymore." Those are just some examples. You must understand that you have to loose the opposite and stop speaking negatively about your life, past failures, family, finances, etc.

Here's an example of what you say instead of being negative about your finances: "Lord, I know we've made mistakes with our finances, but we repent; please forgive us. Now I rebuke and bind the hand of the thief. I loose Your blessing and provision into our lives in the name of Jesus Christ."

Failurism will continue to attach if you continue to speak out and loose the opposite of what's true about you, who you are in Christ, and the authority you walk in. There's power behind our words; therefore, we must speak the right words. Philippians 4:13 says, "I can do all things through Christ who strengthens me" (NKJV). We must know that He is our strength; it comes from Him—not ourselves. We cannot earn it. It is literally this simple: you can do anything through Christ, who gives you the ability to do it. You have to know that this simple verse is powerful!

Breaking Soul Ties

Breaking soul ties is so important. A soul tie is a connection you made with another spiritually. Some soul ties are of God, and some are not. The ties with people God has removed from our lives for our spiritual health would be considered demonic soul ties. Sometimes they can continue to influence us through the open door of a soul tie. Soul ties are not just sexual; they can be created with anyone and used as a witchcraft type of influence over you. Basically, this means that person will still have a measure of control over you and influence you through spiritual manipulation. This turns into baggage you carry around, manipulating your decisions, etc. Examples of these could be old failed relationships, no matter the type: romantic, friendship, or family. It's imperative to break the soul ties connected to failurism.

THE REMOVAL OF SOUL TIES AND BREAKING ATTACHMENTS

Lay hands on yourself and repeat this prayer.

Repent (eyes closed):

> *Dear heavenly Father, I repent for partnering with these soul ties with [insert the people's names]; please forgive me in the name of Jesus Christ.*

Renounce (eyes open):

> *I renounce all soul ties, including with [insert the people's names], and break off any and all attachments they have had on my life. I break all contracts previously made with these soul ties in the name of Jesus Christ of Nazareth.*

Break attachments (eyes open; lay hands on yourself and command the attachment of soul ties to go in the name of Jesus Christ of Nazareth):

> *I break the attachment of soul ties, and I command it to go in the name of Jesus Christ of Nazareth.*

DECLARATION

Say this prayer out loud:

> *I declare Luke 9:1–2 over my life. I declare I've been given power and authority by Jesus Christ to go and cast out demons, to heal the sick, and to seek and save the lost. I declare what I bind on earth shall be bound, and what I loose on earth shall be loosed. From this day forward, I declare that I will walk in the authority given to me, and I will stand firm against the spirit of failurism in my life, in Jesus' name!*

CHAPTER 20

OBEDIENCE IS KEY

ONE OF THE biggest mistakes we make in our walks with Christ is disobedience. We have to be aware that our obedience is key to opening the door to breaking failurism. You're probably thinking, What does obedience have to do with anything? The reality is we have to stop doing the things that God has told us to change. Obedience is a severe spiritual battle, and rebellion is witchcraft. I'm not saying that change is easy or that it doesn't take time and effort, but absolute disobedience to the things God has told you to change or do differently will keep you bound in failurism.

We strip ourselves of power when we are not obedient. We will continue to believe that we are failures, yet the entire time we are just being disobedient. Then we beat ourselves up for being disobedient, and it really shows up as failurism in our lives. It's very important to have power and authority as we walk this Christian walk; we have to be willing to let the Lord lead us in our growth. We have to stop doing what He has told us to change. It is so freeing just to obey and do what God said or asked you to do, even if it's hard at the moment to be obedient. You strip yourself of power if you cannot be obedient. You are saying to the devil, "Go ahead and send failurism right on in." You are giving the failure spirit power over you. The more we obey God's voice and are obedient to Him, the stronger we become—because, once again, it's not by our power or strength. It's by simply obeying Him because Jesus alone is our righteousness. The enemy will bring attacks against us as we are faithful to Christ. It's inevitable. But as long as what we're doing and our direction is in obedience to God and the Holy Spirit, we will be able to walk free of this evil stronghold.

When we are followers of Christ, but we refuse to be obedient to the growth steps He's telling us to make, we feel guilty deep inside, and we live in a place of deep failure. But the cure is always there: simply obey Christ. We can never go wrong by being obedient to Him. Everything He calls us to do, change, or give up is all for His glory and our good. It will produce good fruit, but disobedience and rebellion will not produce good fruit. To be spiritually set free from failurism, you must learn that obedience is key!

> Therefore, to him who knows to do good and does not do it, to him it is sin.
>
> —JAMES 4:17, NKJV

As I said, disobedience is rebellion, and it is like witchcraft. We are basically manipulating our relationships with Christ. We believe that we know better than Christ and the Holy Spirit, but the truth is that the side effect of that belief is the spirit of failurism. Then everything we've discussed in this book has bound you because you would not just do things God's way and trust that He is your strength and Jesus alone is your righteousness. You cannot be righteous on your own. Let's look in *The Message*:

> As it is, you are full of your grandiose selves. All such vaunting self-importance is evil. In fact, if you know the right thing to do and don't do it, that, for you, is evil.
>
> —James 4:16–17, msg

Sometimes I like to look at *The Message* version just to throw in some flair, and it's a little more in your face!

> Be doers of the word and not hearers only, deceiving yourselves.
>
> —James 1:22, mev

As I talked about at the beginning of this book, deception is deceiving. We are deceived when we believe that we can continue without obeying Christ and what He has told us to do. We are deceived when we believe that by disobeying we will find freedom and produce the good fruit that only comes through obedience. It's so relieving to know that what we do and don't do is Christ's decision in our lives. We're letting Him decide. We are set free when we do that, but we don't know it until we become obedient and begin to change. Then we defeat the rebellion and the failurism that comes with rebellion. When we believe that we're free to do what we want when we want and how we want, that's rebellion, not freedom. Rebellion will keep failurism active in your life because you're being reliant on your own plan instead of God's plan for you. That will lead to the downward spiral of the manifestations and symptoms of the spirit of failurism being alive and well in your life. True freedom and peace come through obedience to Christ and the knowledge that we're not responsible for the outcome; He is. Amen! Then we break failurism!

Being doers of the word is not hard when you're doing it in obedience to Christ and the Spirit moving and working through you in power and authority. We defeat failurism by being doers of His word, not doers of our own word, plans, and thoughts.

CHAPTER 21

BE HUMBLE IN SPIRIT

FRANCIS FRANGIPANE ONCE wrote, "Satan fears virtue. He is terrified of humility; he hates it. He sees a humble person, and it sends chills down his back. His hair stands up when Christians kneel down, for humility is the surrender of the soul to God. The devil trembles before the meek because, in the very areas where he once had access, there stands the Lord, and Satan is terrified of Jesus Christ."[1]

We have to stop letting Satan accuse us. What does that mean? When Satan constantly reminds us of our past, sins, and failures, we need to choose humility, not pride. Pride will tell us to build a wall and refuse to accept responsibility for things Satan is accusing us of. Satan is the accuser of the brethren. His goal is to beat us down, which leads to failurism, and keep us in a defensive position or keep us trying to look holier than we are. When we choose this response to his accusations, we are full of pride, not humility. You might think that this doesn't make any sense. Shouldn't we defend ourselves when we are being accused? Isn't that a sign we are trying not to fail or grab on to Satan's lies?

Here are some answers to those questions. First,

being in denial about your past is a spirit of pride and self-righteousness, not a spirit of humility. People often get this confused. Our power comes from a humble spirit, not a spirit of pride and defense. We have to accept the weaknesses that have brought us to the place of needing the salvation and deliverance we received through the power of the cross. Defending ourselves against the accuser actually takes us deeper into our failurism because we are still reliant on our own strength. We can never defeat it in our own strength; Jesus alone is our righteousness. This is where people sit deceived for years because they don't understand that they are not walking in humility. They don't recognize they are still relying on their own strength, and therefore it is not Christ working through them and in them. We must see our need for Christ; it's His power that brings freedom. We can't do anything without Him and His Spirit. Jesus didn't defend Himself:

> And the chief priests accused him of many things. And Pilate again asked him, "Have you no answer to make? See how many charges they bring against you." But Jesus made no further answer, so that Pilate was amazed.
>
> —MARK 15:3–5

Jesus could have gone wild, defended Himself, and called fire down from heaven, but He chose to remain humble and quiet. He didn't argue or flaunt His power or try to prove anything to save His own skin. We can learn so much from this moment with Jesus. Our power comes from Him. Failurism keeps us relying on our righteousness and our ability to look right and good. Those things will fail us over and over. A person with a humble spirit knows they are nothing without Christ. None of their works change anything. Only reliance on Christ and His power affects our lives or how we are meant to work in the lives of others.

So the big question: What is our response when the enemy accuses us night and day? We either say nothing, just as Jesus did, or we agree with the accuser. WHAT? Agree? Why? How is that being humble? Let me explain.

When Satan accuses us, there will always be a little bit of truth to what he says. That is why it hurts and cuts deep. Don't sink to his level; take the high road and choose humility. We will say something like this to the accuser: "Yeppers, I've made plenty of mistakes and hurt others in the process, but I have repented for that, and God has forgiven me. I'm no longer that person, and Christ's power works through me. I am called and chosen, so be silent, devil, in the name of Jesus Christ." A spirit of pride keeps you bound, but humility sets you free. That is a powerful statement! The enemy has no power over you when you walk in humility and know where your ability comes from. It will make it really hard for failurism to take hold and latch on if you walk in a humble spirit because all the lies it tries to feed you won't work. You know you will never be righteous in your own power because *Jesus alone is your righteousness*! Just as the devil asked God if he could sift Job, and God said yes, God will sometimes allow us to be sifted.

> Now there was a day when the sons of God came to present themselves before the LORD, and Satan also came among them. The LORD said to Satan, "From where have you come?" Satan answered the LORD and said, "From going to and fro on the earth, and from walking up and down on it." And the LORD said to Satan, "Have you considered my servant Job, that there is none like him on the earth, a blameless and upright man, who fears God and turns away from evil?" Then Satan answered the LORD and said, "Does Job fear God for no reason? Have you not put a hedge around him and his house and all that he has, on every side? You have blessed the work of his hands, and his possessions have increased in the land. But stretch out your hand and touch all that he has, and he will curse you to your face." And the LORD said to Satan, "Behold, all that he has is in your hand. Only against him do not stretch out your hand." So Satan went out from the presence of the LORD.
>
> —JOB 1:6–12

God allowed Job to be accused by Satan, but Job made it through the testing. Was it easy? No, but the sifting brought Job closer to God and to a better understanding of how God alone is our righteousness. The sifting, or accusing, brings us face to face with our humanity. We, as humans, fail and make mistakes. To remain humble, we must stay aware of that. We are only right through Christ, not our own works.

James 4:10 says, "Humble yourselves before the Lord, and he will exalt you." We don't exalt ourselves. We are to remain humble. Humility is powerful!

PRAYER FOR
THE FORGIVENESS OF PRIDE AND SELF-RIGHTEOUSNESS

Repeat this prayer:

> *Dear heavenly Father, please forgive me for walking in pride and self-righteousness. I renounce the power of pride in my life and break all contracts I've previously made with pride, in the name of Jesus Christ! Lord, I ask You to fill me now with a spirit of humility and meekness and give me the ability to walk humbly every day in every area of my life.*

PART III

PRACTICAL WAYS TO DEFEAT THE SPIRIT OF FAILURISM

CHAPTER 22

TRUST IS KEY

REMEMBER WHEN YOU were first saved, so in love with God, and set ablaze for Him because the salvation He died to give you was so powerful in your life? That salvation kept you going. You were filled with the Holy Spirit and zeal to serve God. We all have this kind of story about when we first accepted Christ. It's God's heart for us to always walk with that fire and never lose our first love.

Revelation 2:4–5 says, "But I have this [charge] against you, that you have left your first love [you have lost the depth of love that you first had for Me]. So remember the heights from which you have fallen, and repent [change your inner self—your old way of thinking, your sinful behavior—seek God's will] and do the works you did at first [when you first knew Me]; otherwise, I will visit you and remove your lampstand (the church, its impact) from its place—unless you repent" (AMP). What exactly was Jesus saying? The church He was addressing had let their fire go out; they had forgotten the first moment they were saved and received the revelation that Jesus Christ was real, and salvation was real and powerful.

Here's how the story usually goes, as we continue to live our lives after we get saved: trouble comes in many forms—satanic attacks and backlash, income loss, job loss, or the loss of a loved one—and when struggles come, we begin to lose our trust in God. We lose the love we once had for all Christ did for us on the cross.

The First Practical Way—Trust God

First on the list of practical ways to defeat failurism is to trust God. Trust in the salvation you received. As we face struggles, we often begin to move away from relying on the fire and power that we walked in when we were first saved, the power that made us fearless! Bold! Crazy! Jesus freaky! Nothing fazes us when we walk with that passion; we trust God with everything and plow through in the glory. To defeat this nasty demon from stealing our lives in Christ, *we must trust in the salvation bought for us on the cross*! We can't move away from that. *Trusting* in the salvation of the cross is the key to all other forms of trust working in our lives. It's the key that opens the door for everything else to be unmovable, unshakable. If we don't lose this knowledge, then the enemy has no power to defeat us. We have to take ourselves back to the foot of the cross daily. The cross is all powerful! Jesus never moves; we move! The further away we move, the easier it is to fall into the trap of judging everything by what our eyes see, becoming complacent, and just barely surviving in your relationship with Christ instead of thriving and growing and producing fruit. We cannot let our salvation lose its power. Ultimately, it's the foundation of everything.

> In this the love of God was made manifest among us, that God sent his only Son into the world, so that we might live through him.
>
> —1 JOHN 4:9

Notice John used the word *live*. Your original salvation cannot lose its *life* or its power to continue to work in you and through you. The devil will have nothing on you if you *live* in the power of your salvation. We can't lose what the cross means: victory. That means if we received *victory* the day we received Christ, we can *trust* that salvation to give us what we need to *live*.

> Behold, God is my salvation; I will trust, and will not be afraid; for the LORD GOD is my strength and my song, and he has become my salvation.
>
> —ISAIAH 12:2

Isaiah is very clear here. Christ has become the salvation of our lives, and we can only exist in Him. *This salvation* is our strength; it's the foundational song of our walks that we never stop singing. If we do, we fall into *not* trusting and then relying on works or what our eyes see. Jesus alone is our righteousness. Salvation is life!

> For in him we live and move and exist. As some of
> your own poets have said, "We are his offspring."
> —ACTS 17:28, NLT

We will stay focused as we trust in our original salvation. Failurism will have no power over us. This also falls under the category of taking authority. Grab hold of that salvation and hold tight with all your strength! The gift you received came with authority. As a believer, you have authority given to you by Christ, and you don't have to fall into failurism and distrust.

> ...even when we were dead in our trespasses,
> made us alive together with Christ—by grace
> you have been saved—and raised us up with him
> and seated us with him in the heavenly places in
> Christ Jesus.
> —EPHESIANS 2:5–6

We have been raised with Him and seated in heaven with Him. There's authority attached to that. As we walk through life, our original salvation has plenty of power to carry us through all this life throws at us. *We must trust it!*

CHAPTER 23

BE FILLED

As we learn to trust the salvation we originally received, we have to know there's much more. Although salvation is number one, we also need to consider our first love. Do you know how you feel when falling in love with your spouse, child, or animal? You are all giddy and can't wait to see and spend all your free time with them.

As we move past salvation into a walk with Christ, God takes us through the sanctification process to remove "us" and fill us with more of Him and His ways. This is a lifelong journey, and the process is beautiful. But there's more beyond the moment we receive Christ. In the same way you couldn't wait to spend time with the love of your life, Christ is eager to spend time with us and wants us to feel the same way about Him. He is our first love, and if we don't want our fire to go out, the second practical way to defeat the spirit of failurism is to *make time for God.*

The Second Practical Way—Make Time for Him

God is a jealous God. Spending time with Him and receiving from His presence is a must to defeat failurism! We are to put Him first in everything.

> So be on your guard and watch yourselves, so that you do not forget the covenant of the LORD your God which He has made with you, and make for yourselves a carved or sculpted image in the form of anything which the LORD your God has forbidden you. For the LORD your God is a consuming fire; He is a jealous (impassioned) God [demanding what is rightfully and uniquely His].
> —DEUTERONOMY 4:23–24, AMP

We cannot forget the day we came into agreement with Christ through salvation. Here God was warning the Israelites to watch themselves and not put anything (idols) above Him. Still, we often get distracted with life's demands, keep up with our responsibilities and struggles, and then spend less time with God over time. But God is a jealous God—the good kind of jealous! He longs to be with us daily. What is so important about this time we set aside? It is when we can learn, grow, repent, and receive from His presence, giving us the strength to walk in power and defeat failurism. Time with God is so special. It's the time we get renewed each day, and we are kept humble by the full knowledge of our need for Him. Time with Him means setting aside the time for worship, prayer, study of His Word, and repentance. Let's break this down.

The Third Practical Way— Setting the Time Aside

Matthew 6:33 says, "But first and most importantly seek (aim at, strive after) His kingdom and His righteousness [His way of doing and being right—the attitude and character of God], and all these things will be given to you also" (AMP). First and foremost, we have to decide whether we will spend time with God, no matter what is going on in our lives or how busy we think we are. As Matthew states, if we put God first and seek His face, God will take care of the rest.

I have many things happening, ministries to run, etc., but God always gets the first three to four hours of each day before I even start ministry work. Of course, not everyone can devote that much time. I'm in a different position as a pastor and prophet and being called to deliverance/healing ministry. But no matter what, everyone can make time for Him. If He is number one in our lives, we will not want to miss one day with Him. I choose early mornings, which work best for my schedule. Some people work nights or evening shifts, so they may have to adjust, but I recommend your morning as the best time, whenever your morning is. Doing it at night before bed is OK, but you need to start your day in His presence and feed on Him. However that works for you, I believe your day should start with time with Him. You can end it with Him too, but honestly, with the distractions of the day and working all day, it's more easily skipped. It's less likely to be ignored if you put Him first before you officially start your day. So *make time*! Paul said in Galatians that the life we live we now live in Him!

> I have been crucified with Christ [that is, in Him I have shared His crucifixion]; it is no longer I who live, but Christ lives in me. The life I now live in the body I live by faith [by adhering to, relying on, and completely trusting] in the Son of God, who loved me and gave Himself up for me.
> —GALATIANS 2:20, AMP

The Fourth Practical Way—Worship

It's essential to start your time with God in worship. Prepare a song list of just worship songs—not the music on Christian radio unless it's worship. Worship songs speak of His greatness, glorify Him, and are full of honor and adoration for Him—not asking for anything or talking about what He's done for you, but just glorifying Him and His holy name. I must emphasize how important it is to welcome His presence and name. His presence is what we draw from to receive our strength and refilling for the day. As you bless God and honor Him, He will bless you with His presence.

Depending on how much time you have, I recommend

starting with twenty minutes of worship. This time can include worshipping in your prayer language if you're baptized in the Holy Spirit, laying on the floor face down humbly before Him, kneeling, or pacing back and forth. King David was a worshipper of worshippers! He danced before the Lord in worship. His wife, the queen, was embarrassed by his act of public worship. Let us not be embarrassed to become a spectacle for all to see as we lift up the King of kings in worship! Here's what David said:

> The LORD reigns; let the peoples tremble! He sits enthroned upon the cherubim; let the earth quake! The LORD is great in Zion; he is exalted over all the peoples. Let them praise your great and awesome name! Holy is he! The King in his might loves justice. You have established equity; you have executed justice and righteousness in Jacob. Exalt the LORD our God; worship at his footstool! Holy is he! Moses and Aaron were among his priests, Samuel also was among those who called upon his name. They called to the LORD, and he answered them. In the pillar of the cloud he spoke to them; they kept his testimonies and the statute that he gave them. O LORD our God, you answered them; you were a forgiving God to them, but an avenger of their

wrongdoings. Exalt the LORD our God, and worship at his holy mountain; for the LORD our God is holy!

—PSALM 99

The Fifth Practical Way—Studying His Word

This is very simple but powerful! We have to be feeding ourselves with God's Word daily. The problem is that we feed on other ungodly things all day, so we need to start the day with God's thoughts and His heart at work in us. How do we study His Word? I say keep it simple! Many do these programs to read the Bible from cover to cover in one year. Those are great, but honestly, meeting a goal defeats the purpose of learning, growing, and taking time to listen to what the Holy Spirit is saying to you. I'm for goals, but your only goal should be to read His Word and hear from Him a beautiful nugget of truth or revelation to teach you His heart and how it relates to you. Only the Holy Spirit can highlight and teach.

If we rush just to meet a goal, then our time isn't for Him, and the reading isn't for Him. It's to pat ourselves on the back for accomplishing the end goal. The point of devotion is receiving from His presence, learning and growing in Him, and knowing Him more; it's not to prove anything. That's religion and a spirit of religion. Spending time with God is about our relationship and learning the Father's heart. Then we act on what He shows us and seek to apply it to our lives to the best of our ability. His Word is a living Word. It is alive and active when we read and apply it. Knowing the Word and understanding the truth of who God is will give you ammo to defeat the spirit of failurism. God's Word is the final word! Amen! Let's look at what Paul told Timothy:

> All Scripture is God-breathed [given by divine inspiration] and is profitable for instruction, for conviction [of sin], for correction [of error and restoration to obedience], for training in righteousness [learning to live in conformity to God's will, both publicly and privately—behaving honorably with personal integrity and moral courage]; so that the man of God may be complete and proficient, outfitted and thoroughly equipped for every good work.
>
> —2 TIMOTHY 3:16–17, AMP

Paul was letting Timothy know we must hold firm the Word of God; the Holy Spirit's anointing and presence is on the words in the Bible. They come directly from the Holy Spirit; what a beautiful gift. God's Word is powerful! I've heard people say we don't need to read God's Word every day—it's not that big of a deal; that's what church is for! Lord, help us if we think that way! Of course, the church is a place to learn, grow, and have fellowship, but your pastor or connect group leader is not responsible for your walk with God. You are. We must feed ourselves and build personal relationships with Christ, which is key to breaking or defeating any oppressive stronghold. Nothing can touch us when we have filled ourselves with God through time spent with Him! The enemy will try, but his power will be minimal. What can the devil do to someone who is fully surrendered to Christ? He can do very little, because we aren't driven by money or idols. The presence of God drives us, and the knowledge of who He is and His passion keeps us going!

The Sixth Practical Way—Prayer

> If my people who are called by my name humble themselves, and pray and seek my face and turn from their wicked ways, then I will hear from heaven and will forgive their sin and heal their land.
>
> —2 CHRONICLES 7:14

Prayer must be the foundation of our lives. Through prayer, we build a two-way relationship with the Holy Spirit, and a two-way conversation can take place. We have to humble ourselves, recognize our need for Him beyond life's needs, and go to Him with everything. Many say, "I can't hear God or don't know how to hear Him." He speaks in many ways, but first and foremost, you must know He is and has always been speaking. Sometimes we don't hear Him because of distractions or other voices that make it hard to hear Him.

Jeremiah 29:12 says, "Then you will call upon me and

come and pray to me, and I will hear you." Learning to build a life of prayer is so important to breaking and defeating failurism. We must know God wants to hear from us. Many say that God can do what He wants, so why do we need to pray? We pray because in doing so, we partner with Him to see His will done on earth.

Ezekiel 3:17 says, "Son of man, I have made you a watchman for the house of Israel. Whenever you hear a word from my mouth, you shall give them warning from me." God has called us to be watchmen. A watchman prays.

> On your walls, O Jerusalem, I have set watchmen;
> all the day and all the night, they shall never be
> silent. You who put the LORD in remembrance, take
> no rest.
>
> —ISAIAH 62:6

We can't be watchmen if we don't realize how important prayer is and that growing and building a prayer life is *valuable*! It's an honor to come before the God of the universe to pray and seek His face and actually be heard! What an amazing gift! We are watchmen of our families, churches, coworkers, the salvation of loved ones, healing and restoration of others, our nation, the world, unborn babies, the hurting and broken, drug addicts, the homeless, abused children, and the list could go on.

Therefore, confess your sins to one another [your false steps, your offenses], and pray for one another, that you may be healed and restored. The heartfelt and persistent prayer of a righteous man (believer) can accomplish much [when put into action and made effective by God—it is dynamic and can have tremendous power].

— JAMES 5:16, AMP

Our prayers matter, and they are powerful! Many times, we won't feel powerful, but our prayers are working! Depending on where you're at in your walk and current prayer life, you will need to decide what works for you. I always recommend keeping it simple if you're getting started. If having a regular prayer life and setting time aside during devotions is new to you, here's how you can begin.

First, decide the length of time. I recommend fifteen minutes. If you aim too long initially, you will get tired or run out of stuff to pray for and feel you failed. That's the opposite of what we want. You can pray for family, friends, and your church family during this time, and making a list is helpful. I believe once you make a list and make your way through, you will use up fifteen minutes pretty quickly. Once you have filled up that time regularly, bump your time up and add five minutes. God doesn't expect you to spend hours in prayer because setting too high expectations of yourself will only cause you to get offended when you can't meet them. (Yes, we can be offended by ourselves.) Then we beat ourselves up for not meeting the expectations we set for ourselves. We can't defeat failurism if our time spent with God is causing us to beat ourselves up. Be realistic. Take one day at a time. Also, if you are baptized in the Holy Spirit and still new to Christ and have a serious devotion, I recommend you pray in your prayer language for five minutes and then do fifteen minutes in your regular language. That helps prime the pump because the Holy Spirit guides your prayers and they become more effective.

If you are not new to this and are more seasoned in the Lord, I will share what I did to grow my prayer life. I would worship for twenty minutes, pray in the spirit for at least ten to fifteen minutes, then go into my Bible time and study God's Word for thirty minutes. Then I would go on a prayer drive for thirty to sixty minutes, pray my prayer list and anything the Holy Spirit brought to my attention while out. Because I move and pray in the prophetic, I'm usually just along for the ride and pray what the Holy Spirit shows me as I go. My routine now—although it usually goes according to what the Holy Spirit is doing—is typically I go into deep worship for an hour, read and study for an hour, and pray in the spirit for an hour; that is a short day.

The Seventh Practical Way—Repentance

What do I mean by repentance? We already talked about that, right? We did address it as part of your spiritual preparation for breaking failurism, but this is different. Being in a place of repentance when spending time with God is a way of saying, "God, I need You. I can't do anything without You. Forgive me for anything that I might have done to offend You; remove these things as I sit in Your presence, Lord." We are not to live in shame or condemnation; that's not what this is. This is a heart posture. You are saying you need God desperately because you are a human with many faults, and you can't become anything without His Word and presence in your life.

CHAPTER 24

START SOMEWHERE

THIS CHAPTER IS short and straightforward: start somewhere. Start doing the things He has told you to do. Start making the changes He has been telling you to make. One sure way to defeat failurism is to start somewhere, one day at a time. Start changing the things the Lord has told you to adjust and work on them. Don't look at it as a huge mountain that must be moved. Take one day at a time and start somewhere.

> And He was also telling them a parable: "No one tears a piece of cloth from a new garment and puts it on an old garment; otherwise he will both tear the new, and the piece from the new will not match the old. And no one puts new wine into old wineskins; otherwise the new wine will burst the skins and it will be spilled out, and the skins will be ruined. But new wine must be put into fresh wineskins."
>
> —LUKE 5:36–38, NASB

As you can see by this passage, we have to have a new start. We must plan to do something new, go in a new direction to see changes, and not let failurism attach to us. We have to understand that we can't keep doing the old things we've been doing, which would represent the old piece of garment, and expect a different outcome than what we've already had. Don't set yourself up for more failure by setting a goal or expectation for yourself. Take it one day at a time because there is massive freedom in this. Do the things He's already told you to change. Little by little, the demon of failurism will have no power when you're working toward changing the things that you've failed at in the past or felt you weren't making progress in. You can't use old activities and old behaviors to change into something new. We have to have a fresh new direction to have a different outcome.

Maybe the Lord has been telling you to get your house cleaned and organized, change jobs, step away from wrong relationships and friendships, get your finances in order, start tithing, etc. You tie His hands until you start working toward what He said to change. We don't have to sit in darkness. The light has been made available to shine on those in darkness. We have to choose to step into the light; change is the light. Start somewhere!

CHAPTER 25

DEFEATING FAILURISM HINGES ON ONE THING!

When I first began walking in the anointing and impartation, men of God laid hands on me, which activated my spiritual gifts and brought all that God was calling me to do to the surface "for such a time as this" (Esther 4:14). It was very hard to be obedient to the call at the time. I struggled to believe I could actually do it, that He had chosen me to be a glory carrier and to bring miracles of healing, deliverance, and freedom to people. I had been through many rejections and had become works oriented without knowing.

James 2:26 says that "faith without works is dead" (NKJV), so works and serving are something we should be doing. However, when we become reliant on the works—whether we feel the need to gain approval because of previous rejection or just because of growing up in this world—it's easy to begin to think we're the ones with the power to accomplish everything and make a difference. Because of this thought process, I had no faith in what God was calling me to do. I had been serving God, was always on fire, and was full of passion, but as soon as I was responsible for bringing healing or miracles and seeing a God-only outcome, I felt unable to do it. I asked God daily, "Why me?" but in a good way. I told the Lord I was humbled and honored to be chosen and anointed. Still, I was beyond afraid of walking it out and afraid of failing. I asked God, "How will I ever be able to do this?"

He said, "It will never be you. I'm the One doing it through you; it will never be you or your works!"

I was like, "Glory bomb, massive revelation!" The glory fell, and boom! I can't fail when it is not me but Him doing it. He's responsible for the result. I'm only responsible for walking out the calling and being a willing vessel in obedience to the anointing.

Satan plays the same game with failurism. He tries to deceive us into thinking we have the power to do what only God can do. Throughout this book, the big revelation or message is this: Jesus alone is our righteousness! As I've mentioned several times, He alone is righteous. We are only right through Him and because of Him. While the spirit of failurism has many other strongholds and demons attached that need removal so we can be set free, the main revelation of this entire book is *Jesus alone is our righteousness*. We often believe we have some power to control all outcomes, and our works or behavior will make us righteous. That's the big lie of this spirit, which is the open door that allows failurism to attach to us and begin its oppressive process.

The lie of this spirit opens the door, allowing failurism to attach and begin its oppressive process. This spirit wants us to control the things we have no control over. That gives us all the power and control over the physical and spiritual outcomes being good or right. This sounds fun and awesome when you're allowing that power to drive you, but it is not fun when you fail and can't pick yourself back up because you're basing the ability to change yourself or others on your own limited works. But Jesus alone is our righteousness. When we beat ourselves up for our failures, mistakes, or even sin, we have to know we only have so much power. But if we accept God's forgiveness and that we are righteous through Him and Him alone, then we won't fall into the pattern of the spirit of failurism.

Let us read this excerpt from Francis Frangipane's book *Holiness, Truth, and the Presence of God*:

> Let me share an experience. A certain man of God had been gifted with revelatory insight into people's lives. During an evening service he ministered to a Presbyterian pastor and his wife. By the gift of the Spirit, he revealed the couple's past, uncovered their present situation, and then disclosed to them what was to come. This work of God greatly impressed the couple, and as the prophecies were fulfilled, one month later the Presbyterian minister brought two other pastors,

each with their wives, to another service for personal ministry.

The word of knowledge was exceptionally sure that night, and the second minister and his wife marveled at the accuracy and truth in the prophetic word. The third couple stepped forward for ministry, and again the word of knowledge was present. The prophet spoke to the husband, revealing his past, present, and insight into his future. Then the man of God turned to this third minister's wife. As he began to speak of her past, suddenly he stopped. "There was a very serious sin in your past." The woman, with her worst fear upon her, turned pale and closed her eyes. The congregation hushed and moved to the edge of their seats.

The prophet continued, "And I asked the Lord, 'What was this sin that she committed?' And the Lord answered, *'I don't remember!'*"[1]

Amen! This story is awesome! We have to know we are forgiven the same way, and our sins are remembered no more. When we fail and ask for forgiveness, we are forgiven and made right in and through Christ.

And you, being dead in your trespasses and the uncircumcision of your flesh, He has made alive together with Him, having forgiven you all trespasses, having wiped out the handwriting of requirements that was against us, which was contrary to us. And He has taken it out of the way, having nailed it to the cross.

—COLOSSIANS 2:13–14, NKJV

Boom! It's been nailed to the cross. Am I saying this cures you of ever failing? Of course not! We all will fail, sin, and make mistakes, but it's how we handle them. Do we ask for forgiveness and allow God to nail them to the cross? Do we understand that no matter what, we will never be holy and pure enough on our own, but we are made right through Him? Do we trust in what has been made right? Do we believe Christ's love can cover a multitude of sins? (See 1 Peter 4:8.) We must be able to answer with a huge resounding *yes!* And then we must believe it and carry it with us and in us. This will stop the spirit of failurism from having the power or ability to attach and wreak havoc in your life. Failurism will literally destroy your life.

Now that we have been put right with God through faith, we have peace with God through our Lord Jesus Christ.

—ROMANS 5:1, GNT

You notice this verse says faith is what makes us right with God. We must believe that His righteousness is enough, and all self-reliance or human ability has to be replaced with our faith in the finished work of the cross in our lives.

> Nevertheless, I am continually with you; you
> hold my right hand. You guide me with your
> counsel, and afterward you will receive me to
> glory. Whom have I in heaven but you? And
> there is nothing on earth that I desire besides
> you. My flesh and my heart may fail, but God is
> the strength of my heart and my portion forever.
>
> —PSALM 73:23–26

The psalmist expresses it perfectly! He is our strength, and it will never be our own strength that saves us. We were received in glory at the time of salvation. Who we are is found in Him, our gifts and abilities are only found in Him, and who we are in Christ is only found in Him. Our works or deeds are as filthy rags.

> But we are all like an unclean thing, and all our
> righteousnesses are like filthy rags; we all fade
> as a leaf, and our iniquities, like the wind, have
> taken us away.
>
> —ISAIAH 64:6, NKJV

You're probably thinking, "Ouch! That's harsh!" This is reality; we must know our holiness is only from and through Him.

> But when the kindness and the love of God our
> Savior toward man appeared, not by works of
> righteousness which we have done, but according

to His mercy He saved us, through the washing
of regeneration and renewing of the Holy Spirit.
—TITUS 3:4–5, NKJV

This is a huge relief!! Let this settle in your spirit: it is
not by our works, the good things we try to do. We are
already being made right through Him! Amen!

Jesus alone is our righteousness! Failurism will lose all
power as you walk in this revelation. It will still try to
mess with you, but eventually it will lose its power.

NOTES

Chapter 1

1. *Merriam-Webster*, s.v. "failing," accessed January 24, 2023, https://www.merriam-webster.com/dictionary/failing.
2. *Merriam-Webster*, s.v. "failure," accessed January 24, 2023, https://www.merriam-webster.com/dictionary/failure.
3. *Vine's Expository Dictionary of NT Words*, s.v. "fail," StudyLight, accessed January 24, 2023, https://www.studylight.org/dictionaries/eng/ved/f/fail.html.
4. *Merriam-Webster*, s.v. "ism," accessed January 24, 2023, https://www.merriam-webster.com/dictionary/ism.
5. Urban Dictionary, s.v. "-ism," accessed January 24, 2023, https://www.urbandictionary.com/define.php?term=Isming.

Chapter 2

1. *Merriam-Webster*, s.v. "deception," accessed January 24, 2023, https://www.merriam-webster.com/dictionary/deception.
2. *International Standard Bible Encyclopedia*, s.v. "deceivableness; deceive," accessed January 27, 2023, https://www.internationalstandardbible.com/D/deceivableness-deceive.html.

Chapter 10

1. John Bevere, *The Bait of Satan* (Lake Mary, FL: Charisma House, 2014), 15.

Chapter 16

1. *Merriam-Webster*, s.v. "aimless," accessed January 24, 2023, https://www.merriam-webster.com/dictionary/aimless.

Chapter 18

1. *Merriam-Webster*, s.v. "unbelief," accessed January 24, 2023, https://www.merriam-webster.com/dictionary/unbelief.
2. Blue Letter Bible, s.v. "*apistia*," accessed February 2, 2023, https://www.blueletterbible.org/lexicon/g570/kjv/tr/0-1/.

Chapter 19

1. *King James Dictionary*, s.v. "rebuke," Bible Study Tools, accessed February 2, 2023, https://www.biblestudytools.com/dictionaries/king-james-dictionary/rebuke.html.

Chapter 21

1. Francis Frangipane, *Strength for the Battle* (Lake Mary, FL: Charisma House, 2017), 19.

Chapter 25

1. Francis Frangipane, *Holiness, Truth, and the Presence of God* (Lake Mary, FL: Charisma House, 2011), 34–35.

ABOUT THE AUTHOR

Liberty Turnipseed founded Spirit Move Ministry, an apostolic prophetic ministry, in 2018 and built upon it through YouTube, creating Spirit Move Church.

Liberty travels the United States with her husband, children, and team while ministering to the body of Christ through miracles, healings, revivals, the impartation of fire, mass baptisms, and prayer summits. They speak and prophesy over territories and regions.

Liberty has received several impartations of fire that have led to the anointing she carries. As a glory carrier, she seeks to expand the kingdom of God by setting the world on fire by the power of the Holy Spirit!

Liberty is an ordained pastor with the Assemblies of God. She also founded Restoration Deliverance Ministry, Covenant Prayer Movement, Spirit Move School of the Supernatural, and Hopes Community Food Pantry.

For more information, other messages and teachings from Liberty, or to contact her ministry, contact:

Spirit Move Ministry
(817) 349-8799
spiritmoveministry@gmail.com

Spirit Move Church: info@spiritmove.church
Restoration Deliverance Ministry:
restorationfreedom@gmail.com

You can also visit her website, get in touch, and get
more teaching online at www.spiritmove.church or
www.spiritmoveministry.co.